What Readers Are S...

"Terri, you are an amazing teacher!…every time I read a post or hear a talk by you, my life is enriched immensely! This one made my monitor blurry!…I pray I can be as good a friend as you are to your friends, and with your example, I have a good chance to be one!…"

—Maureen Hanratty

"…Thank you for opening this window, and for sharing what must certainly be an emotional roller coaster for you. You inspire us with your faith, positive attitude, and servant heart.…"

—Kevin Dick

"…A book of hope. A book of how a godly woman faces incredible challenges that NO ONE even imagined were so awful. Wow. I'm blown away and glorifying God all at the same time.…"

—Kristine Militello

From the backseat of the car on the way to Pennsylvania today: "Cows smell like number two because they don't wipe." —J.R. (age six)

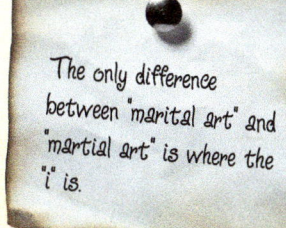

"Your story of your journey of pain, frustration, and pursuit for answers…is incredible!…Because you've been so transparent, others will gain strength and hope for whatever difficulties they are going through.…I can't wait to read [more]—and everyone is right; Chris is NOT the only bestselling author in your house!…"

—Nancy Crumback

"Thank you so much for your stories—and reminders—to have a sense of humor as a Mom.☺ I…appreciate the reminder that sometimes the best thing is to simply laugh!"

—Olivia Shaw

"WOW! I feel God's loving presence as I read your post. Thank you for letting us in in your life experiences, for sharing God's messages through them. You are truly His child and you do Him glory every time you share.…"

—Maribel Damphousse

The only difference between "marital art" and "martial art" is where the "i" is.

"I am a MAN, I read your blog regularly and I am not ashamed. I love the stories and the art, which is your writing style. The way you weave the basket with encouraging words, vulnerable moments and scripture is mind blowing to me and always makes me look inward for things to change. So, thank you from a MAN."

—Michael J. Wilson

Letters to Lindsey

Terri Brady

All rights reserved. No part of this book may be reproduced or transmitted in any form or by any means, electronic or mechanical, including photocopying, recording, or by any information storage and retrieval system, without the written permission of Obstaclés Press. Inquiries should be sent to the publisher.

Obstaclés and the Obstaclés logo are trademarks of The Life Platform
Second Edition, July 2024

Published by:

Obstaclés Press
200 Commonwealth Ct, Cary NC 27511

Copyright © 2013 by The Life Platform

Unless otherwise noted, all Scripture quotations are taken from the *New American Standard Bible* (NASB), copyright 1960, 1962, 1963, 1971, 1972, 1973, 1975, 1977 by The Lockman Foundation. Used by permission. All rights reserved.

Scripture quotations marked NIV are from the *Holy Bible, New International Version* (NIV), copyright 1973, 1978, 1984, 2011 by Biblica, Inc. All rights reserved.

Scripture quotations marked NLT are taken from the *Holy Bible, New Living Translation* (NLT), copyright 1996. Used by permission of Tyndale House Publishers Inc., Wheaton, IL 60189 USA. All rights reserved.

ISBN 979-8-218-47876-6

Portrait photograph of Terri Brady by Steve Kendall
Easter Morning colored-pencil artwork on page 91 by Nicole Avereyn

Cover and layout design by Norm Williams, nwa-inc.com

terribradyblog.com
LettersToLindsey.com

Printed in the United States of America

This book is dedicated to my Lord and Savior, Jesus Christ, and to my family with whom He blessed me. May Chris, Casey, Nate, Christine, J.R., and I return our lives to Him, fully used, for His glory.

Contents

About This Book by Chris Brady 9
Foreword by Laurie Woodward 11
Introduction 13

163 Miles North 15
Buffaloes and Butterflies 18
Are You a Basket Case? 20
Fire! Fire! Pants on Fire! 22
If I Am to Be Queen, I Shall Be a Good One 23
Bad Queens 26
A Stone's Throw 32
Miscarriages and Slow Toddlers 34
Tea Party with a Fashionista 36
Message from the Massage: Good Luck with That! 38
Hard to Swallow 41
Holland or Italy: Just Passing Through 42
Act like the Mom! 45
The Gift That Says, "I'm the Big One!" 48
It Began as a Walk in the Park 51
Throwing Myself under the (School) Bus 57
Homeschooling Missing Ingredients (Mistakes I've Made) 66
Huffin' and Puffin' 71
Turkey Tastes Better without Lily Pads 72
Wanna Talk about Me! 76
Small Enough to Be Used (Whose Baby Is This?!) 80
The Most Difficult Instrumentalist to Find 83
Stop in the Name of the Law 86
Climb the Ladder 89
"I'm Glad I'm a Boy!" 93
Keep Planting 94
Raising Readers 97
"Mom, I Bet You Can*NOT* Do It" 103
Our Turn to Listen 105

Out of My Mind (with a Brain Tumor) Part I 106
Out of My Mind (with a Brain Tumor) Part II 113
Out of My Mind (with a Brain Tumor) Part III 120
Tumor Humor: Out of My Mind (with a Brain Tumor) Part IV 127
Thanks Again 129
"Mom, I Need the Bug Swatter Thing." 130
Wet Light Fixtures and Oatmeal Kisses 131
Coyotes and Jesus 133
When We Don't See a Purpose 135
Crucify Him! (the Song) 140
Blessings That Stick 144
"Call Mom!" 148
Canine Quandary 149
Cat Aversion 153
City Slicker Farming 154
Dampened Impressions, Toddler Style 156
Donating through Dinner, Kick-Starting the Heart 158
Duh, Mom 162
Hold It Down! 163
Random Thoughts of a Child 164
Honesty: Uncovering 10:08s 166
Art Exchange 168
Short, Sweet Prayer 173
Valentine's Posing Pansies 174
Whippoorwill Wakening 177
Balloon Ride to Rome (Love at Every Altitude) 179
Be Still!—for Your Ears' Sake 182
Always? 185
And to My Listening Ear 189
Shine on a Parade 193
Sunrise, Sunset—Fishing for Memories 197
The Ring 200
Acknowledgments 204
Notes 206
About the Author 207

About This Book

I believe some of the best books happen by accident. In this particular case, the author was in total ignorance of the project until a mere month before it went to print. It was once said of Thomas Jefferson regarding the Constitutional Convention that it was a good thing he was in France at the time; otherwise, he would have done his best to put the kibosh on the whole thing. I believe the same would have happened with this book. The project had to go from conception to rough draft, including artistic layouts and concepts, before the original author of the content was allowed to find out about it. Only at that point was there a chance that the official look and feel of the manuscript would provide enough momentum to see the project through any resistance offered by the author. If she had been apprised of the undertaking at any earlier point in the process, the entire project ran the risk of being plucked like a weed sprout in a manicured garden.

Allow me to explain.

Terri Brady, my incredible wife, began writing a blog at the request of several people who had enjoyed her speeches over the course of nearly twenty years. Whether the topic was success, motherhood, Godly living, or overcoming life's obstacles (in her case: infertility, a child with life-threatening food allergies, a brain tumor, and the always daunting task of being my spouse), her captivating approach to teaching through stories, humor, and the joys of raising children struck a chord with audiences around the world. Finally giving in to these requests, Terri hesitantly began writing the blog (www.terribradyblog.com) after a friend, Lindsey Spiewak, encouraged her. Terri felt more comfortable writing in letter form, hence the title *Letters to Lindsey*. In each article, a woman blossoming in motherhood and faithful living gives insights and advice to a younger woman a short way behind her on the same journey. The blog, begun with a wince of reluctance, also quickly caught fire. At the time of this writing, it receives tens of thousands of hits a month, and has been read in 134 countries. Truly, Terri's material had once again found its audience.

Next began the requests by readers and fans that Terri write a book. Humble to the core, she reacted by kindly deflecting the sentiment and saying that I, her husband, was the author of the family and why didn't they simply read my books instead? Nice try. Soon, it became obvious to many of us that Terri's blog was chock full of the kind of material that would be absolutely perfect for a book. Thus began the project of the difficult task of paring Terri's prolific output down to just "the best" content. There is enough quality material available for three books, let alone one. However, in the interest of producing a manageable and approachable book for a wide range of readers, a letter-by-letter selection was finally made.

Enter Terri.

When she found out about the project, her first reaction was a sincere request for it to be canceled. For this, we had been prepared, and she was, in the end, no match for the countermeasures we had planned out in advance. What resulted was her tentative approval, followed by a curious involvement, culminating with a flair of her input that took our concept for the book to entirely new heights. It is very safe to say that without Terri's involvement that last month of creation, the book would be significantly less than it ended up becoming. As a result, what you hold in your hands is a true work of art.

Being married to someone for twenty years is likely the best seat in life's theatre from which to witness the performance of his or her life. From that vantage point, one gets to see the spouse's heart, sincerity, character, and makeup unadorned, as it really is. It is encouraging to me that from such a position, I have consistently grown in my respect for Terri over the years. She is in private what she appears to be in public. She cares deeply about people and about glorifying her Savior. She holds herself to a high standard and is harder on herself than she ever is on anyone else. She strives mightily to not only study her Bible, but to live it. She radiates Christian joy in the face of suffering, never mumbles a "poor me," and greets each day with gratitude and thankfulness. She serves. She studies. She leads. She works. Most of all though, she loves. Our four children and I are the blessed recipients of all that this Godly woman has to offer. Now, we get to share her with you. This book will be a blessing because of what's in it, but even more so because of who is behind it. I hope you enjoy it. I also hope it changes you. Terri would say that the entire project would be in vain if it failed to bring you closer to Christ. May these pages bring you spiritual nourishment and encouragement in your walk with Him.

Chris Brady
New York Times Bestselling Author
(Husband to future bestselling author, Terri Brady)

Foreword

In today's high-tech, media-drenched world, there are many blogs that fight for our attention. There are blogs that teach us how to cook and ones that give us medical, parenting, and marriage advice. There are blogs that teach us how to fix our phones, computers, and pretty much anything else. There are blogs on leadership, politics, and religion. And there are even blogs that teach us how to blog! The list goes on and on. But not every blog is created equal. Some talk straight to the heart and change lives. That is exactly what *Letters to Lindsey* does.

In fact, Terri's whole life story speaks straight to the heart. When I first met her twenty years ago, I knew there was something uniquely special about her. She could tell a story and have you sitting on the edge of your seat anxiously waiting to hear what would happen next! Over the years, that feeling has grown as I have seen her overcome obstacles that would have knocked most people down for the count. I believe Terri's composure and inner strength were developed by looking at the world through a different kind of lens and finding the best in every situation.

When she started writing her blog *Letters to Lindsey*, I knew her readers were in for some fascinating, some heart-wrenching, and some good, old-fashioned, fun stories. More importantly, they were in for some great lessons on life. In each story, Terri takes experiences from her life and unpacks the life principles to be learned from them. In other words, she provides readers the wisdom without having to experience the pain because her stories capture the imagination and make it easy to recognize and remember the wisdom within.

Terri Brady has an amazing talent for taking the ordinary, everyday experiences of life—from snakes in the garage to construction signs to a day of fishing with her son—and turning them into extraordinary life lessons. Terri encapsulates the lessons God gives her in a way that only she can. She makes you laugh, and she makes you cry—sometimes within the same story! And all the while, she is sneaking the lessons she has learned into your heart.

I have also watched Terri go through some extremely unordinary, painful experiences and still have the heart to share her lessons with others. Her wisdom, in a word, is a direct product of her willingness to submit to God's will.

Letters to Lindsey is a unique book that covers a wide array of topics. It is a book on leadership, marriage, parenting, character, freedom, faith, and many other subjects. It is a collection of blog articles written from the heart to touch, and sometimes change, the heart. So sit back and get ready to laugh, cry, and learn.

Laurie Woodward
Founder of the Life Platform

Introduction

My life as a mom, wife, and Christian can be such a blessing—so stressful and so funny all in the same day. After my sons' soccer coaches had changed the location and time of one night's practices twice, my daughter's try-outs were listed on a date that didn't exist, and I happened to notice an error on my son's medical record, I said to my husband in frustration, "How do dumb people be moms?!" He laughed hysterically (probably at my English) and then told me, "THAT's why you need to write!" There are brilliant women putting degrees and the accolades of the world aside in order to keep a family running—with or without another job to juggle at the same time. In no small part, this book is meant as a tribute to them.

Our actions and reactions in life begin with seeds that grow from our thoughts. For this reason, we need to guide our thoughts carefully. One way to do so is to associate with others who are experiencing the same things in order to learn and encourage mutually. In other words, we need to stick together! What mother hasn't wondered from time to time, "Am I the only mom who feels this crazy—in love, crazy—out of control, and crazy—sad they will grow up soon?"

The pages that follow were born out of this double inclination: a salute to motherhood and amazement at what is often required. The stories come mostly from my "ordinary everyday life," which I never feel is "ordinary" (unless you are used to underwear on fire on a chandelier, a fig tree sticking out of a convertible, and finding drawers full of wet, folded clothes). The starring roles of these stories are usually played by my children, Casey (sixteen), Nate (thirteen), Christine (nine), and J.R. (eight), but let's not forget the dog, Delilah (two). Take note, however, that each of these characters was not always these ages, and throughout this book, I will sometimes make reference to them merely by their age at the time of mention. Since I myself confuse their names at times (often when attempting to quickly correct one of them for something), I will not expect you to follow who is who. Instead, their gender and age will often be all that's given to provide the proper setting and action.

Why *Letters to Lindsey*? My friend Lindsey asked me at just the right time if I had ever thought about writing a blog. Thinking she might be the only one who would read it, I decided to write letters to her, but I LOVE that others have enjoyed reading them too! I guess life is full of surprises—including the surprise of this book being compiled. If you didn't happen to read the About This Book section by my husband, author and businessman Chris Brady, then you need to know that much of this book was created behind my back! My husband and some very kind people hatched the plan of taking my most popular blog articles and compiling them into a readable book format. Only at the end of the process was I let in on the game! Reluctant at first, I am now excited at what, through the efforts of some very talented people, has resulted.

It is my hope that you will enjoy these pages from our journey with four children, including some flashbacks to their toddler days (when I had NO TIME for writing)! It is through these experiences with children that I hope to take you closer to the Father. These letters are meant to vent, challenge, or simply entertain, but always to leave the reader *and the writer* changed. By definition, growth cannot occur without change, so I hope that through changing, we are growing to our own highest potential, for His glory.

May God bless our time together.

Sincerely,

Terri Brady

163 Miles North

Dear Lindsey,

The steering wheel was wet. I could barely hold on, but the anger inside seethed and prevented me from stopping, despite my blurred vision from the tears that jumped from my face. I ranted and raved in my head. *The injustice! The money lost! The months waiting! The painful nights! The fervent prayers…all for nothing!*

I drove north from the fertility doctor's office in Ann Arbor, Michigan, in a silent car that was full of noise. In forty-five minutes, I would be telling Chris that it didn't work. It was the end of the line. "You can wait a year and try again," the nurse had consoled.

Does she know how long twelve months is?!

We were at the end of the line of treatments. Four years into marriage, and nine years into female issues, I had tried the pills, the surgeries, the shots, and now a mixture of them all. "Your best bet is to do this procedure within six months of the surgery," the doctor had said. We had saved the thousands of dollars needed for a chance to have our own child; it would be worth it! We had only spent 20% (in meds), when they told me my body wasn't responding like a twenty-six-year-old's should. "Take the shots for one more month, and it will do the trick," they said. After another yearlong month of being a chemist mixing meds at home and waking Chris early so he could administer them before I left for my engineering job, I guess "the trick" wasn't done. The ultrasound showed only one egg. "There's not enough of a chance of in-vitro working with just one egg to extract," the specialist said. "You can save the rest of your money, and we can try again in a year."

As I drove, it was as if the devil sat on my shoulder and whispered in my ear. My anger turned into a deep sadness. Negative thoughts enveloped me.

You are unworthy of being a mom.
 Don't you remember the things you have done?

Other women would raise children better; God is leaving the job to them. Chris could have married anyone who would have given him a child by now. Maybe he should just go do that.

The tears flowed.

I passed my highway exit, intentionally. I couldn't bear to tell Chris that we had to wait another year. I really knew deep down that another year didn't mean better chances. I would be doing the same thing and expecting a different result: the definition of insanity.

> *Mother's Day: I sent some emotional prayers today for those who wish they were moms and for those who are missing their moms. (1 Chron. 16:11)*

In my despair, I lifted my eyes. I wish I could say it was in a proper way, but I lifted my eyes with more emotion than I have ever experienced "at" God. "Lord, what is this? I *prayed* to You! I had *the dream*. Wasn't that You practically *telling* me that I would be a mom?!"

I had had "the dream" a few weeks prior. I had dreamt I gave birth. In the dream, as I held my new little boy while Chris stood beside me, we thanked God for answering our prayers. I cradled him in the crook of my left arm, as tears flowed down my cheeks and hit the baby's. I told him how we had been waiting for him for so long, and God had answered our prayers. But I awoke on a wet pillow; real tears had been falling from my sleeping body. As I sat up in bed, the weight of disappointment hit when I realized it had only been a dream. The crook of my elbow was still damp with sweat due to the heat of the imagined baby's head. It had been so…real. I wept in bed again, this time in sorrow.

"You gave me such hope," my raging in the car continued, "—all to lead me down this path of pain and emotion, and still no baby? This is torture! I *told* You I didn't want to go through all of that for nothing! I *told* You I wanted to bring You glory by Your healing my infertility…that if You wanted me to adopt, I was fine with it. Why didn't You tell me that it wasn't going to work? I would never have gone through all of this. I wanted *Thy will, not my will!*"

…And it hit me like a ton of bricks. He *had* just told me. Actually, the doctor had just told me. God's will was that the medical procedures would not work. Period.

But what really hit me was that if I was screaming, "*Thy will, not my will!*" at the same time as I was crying, then I was missing the whole point. *My* will is what was causing the tears, the anger, and the sorrow. The deep torture was self-inflicted, as I was refusing to truly surrender. It was as though I thought I could secretly harbor the feelings of how badly I wanted and *deserved* to be a mother, and God wouldn't know. Ha! God wouldn't know? That's just funny. He knew all along.

He knew my love for children as I babysat for over sixty families in high school. He knew my desire to be a good mom, as I told the Pittsburgh newspaper reporter who had asked why an engineering student like me would choose to work at a childcare center to help pay for college. He knew my sinful jealousy when unplanned pregnancies surrounded me. He knew my righteous indignation when a bad parenting story came on the news. He knew I thought I was in control of my life.

And He knew what I needed in order to truly surrender to His will. He was answering my prayers of His will, not mine, and I almost missed it in my emotions.

"Infertility" in life can take many forms—anytime things go in a direction that is opposite from that of our desires, and we are simply left waiting. *But in order for anything to be filled, it must first be emptied.* I believe the infertility was the key to my being emptied and, therefore, the key to being filled.

On my drive that day, a peace came over me, and true silence filled the car. Nature outside came alive as I recognized white birch trees lining both sides of the highway.

"Birch trees? Where am I?" Looking to the first sign, which read, "Mackinac Island 37 miles," I realized I was 163 miles past my exit. Wow. What a car ride! I think Jesus had taken the wheel.

Two weeks later, we found out we were pregnant.

When the doctor recognized me in the parking lot, he excitedly said, "You have been the talk of the board meeting among doctors this week. *One* egg! I guess sometimes nature prevails when science fails."

The womb that had been empty was filled. My heart, which had been filled with *my* will, was emptied—only to be filled again by Him. To God be the glory.

My favorite book, Elizabeth Prentiss's *Stepping Heavenward*, which is a woman's journal, says it this way: "Thus I have been emptied from vessel to vessel, till I have learned that he only is truly happy who has no longer a choice of his own and lies passive in God's hand."[1]

He only is truly happy who says, "Thy will, not my will, be done."

Psalm 51:17—"The sacrifices of God are a broken spirit: a broken and a contrite heart, O God, Thou wilt not despise."

Amen.

Love,

Terri

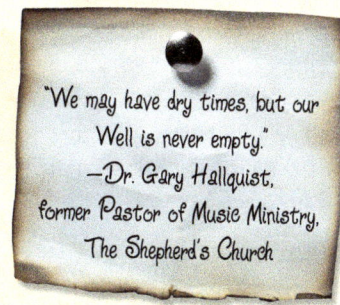

> "We may have dry times, but our Well is never empty."
> —Dr. Gary Hallquist, former Pastor of Music Ministry, The Shepherd's Church

Buffaloes and Butterflies

Dear Lindsey,

When God gave me my little butterfly after my buffaloes, I remember thinking, *Really? You think I can raise a daughter?!*

Every book I read, I relate more to the men's side. I *am* from Mars. (Women are supposed to be from Venus.)[2] I *am* more like waffles. (Women are supposed to be like spaghetti.)[3] And I *am* a buffalo. God gave me a butterfly?[4]

Butterflies are beautiful! They pollinate the flowers, spreading the beauty. Of course, to my disdain, they're dainty and stop flying at the slightest little offense. Christine (age eight) fits the bill! She told me just last week, "Mommy, you should try a brighter lipstick. It would bring out your eyes." She has rarely worn anything but a dress because it's all about "the look," something I have yet to get—as she has pointed out.

> When my daughter saw me researching spring sports options for her, she asked if there was one where she could learn "spa" skills.

Once when she was three, I took her to a nail salon—her dream! She asked if she could sing for the lady next to us. She went from woman to woman, "pollinating" the entire waiting room. The smiles kept multiplying! But a little dust off her wing, and she is down for the count. My favorite was the night she woke me wailing from the top of the stairs, "Mommy! I have music in my no…oh…oh…oh…ose [her nose]!"

She had the sniffles. (I think she meant to say "mucus.")

> "'What the heck?!' is like a fancy way of saying, 'What on earth?'"
> —Christine (age seven)

Buffaloes, on the other hand, are tough-skinned, hard to pierce. They can carry a load like no other. Unfortunately, like a bull in a china shop, they can do damage simply by walking, unaware of the trail of destruction behind them. As a tomboy child, I braved the mean dogs by feeding them live locusts to keep my fearful brothers safe. Seriously. The buffalo in me wore an imaginary badge that said, "You can't hurt me." When in pain, I figured it was weakness that didn't need to be shown! I protected myself with a coat of humor, which hurt everyone around me, breaking the dainty down, one by one, without my noticing! I shudder to think of the more recent times when my daughter waited by the door for my return, holding her beautifully hand-made picture so she could make a glorious presentation, but I, unknowingly, charged past and asked, *"Who made this mess?!"*

While admiring my grown-up butterfly girlfriends' "pollinating" smiles and friends surrounding them, I really *wanted* that. Rather than looking down on them, maybe I needed to recognize their strengths and *emulate* them!

When dealing with relationship problems, I began to see some of my buffalo weaknesses. Maybe instead of blaming others for being so sensitive, I needed to gain some of their ability to sense! By saying, "You can't hurt me," I was really saying, "You can't know me," too. Praying the Lord would reveal my blind spots to me, I was able to open my heart to others and even see a glimpse of how I was hurting them. I finally felt the hurting myself. No polishing occurs without friction, and thanks to that friction within, my buffalo was beginning a kind of metamorphosis.

Now, I have come to the conclusion that to have friends and keep friends, butterfly qualities of "flying high" and "pollinating" must be respected and emulated! Yet, to accomplish anything with excellence, the buffalo's strengths of load-carrying and tough skin are required. Respectful of the strengths of both, I am able to become all God created me to be…in essence, a buffafly.

Love,

Terri

> "Mommy, these eye shadows I got at the Dollar Store are so beautiful you are going to want to borrow them!" —Christine (age eight)

> "Trying to be a buffalo is a waste of a buffafly." —Me

> "Trying to be a man is a waste of a woman." —Movie: *She Can Do It ALL*

> "HOW ARE YOU SUPPOSED TO FROST A COOKIE WITHOUT BREAKING IT?!" said my buffalo Nate (age twelve).

> Every minute spent on stressing rules to someone else is more likely a deterrent from allowing them the relationship with God.

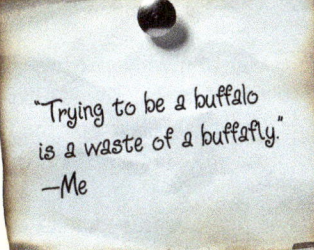

Are You a Basket Case?

Dear Lindsey,

Have you ever had one of those nights when you can't sleep? There have been times when I have fallen asleep in exhaustion, only to lie awake a few hours later because the conflicting thoughts were back into my head. 2:18 a.m., 3:18, 4:18...*Maybe I should just get up. No! I'm tired!* Then I finally doze off just before the morning alarm rings and wonder, *Did I ever sleep?* I think my body collapsed but my mind stayed vigilant *all night.*

After moving to a new state, I went to a general practitioner for a "meet the doctor" appointment, and I'll never forget one of the questions he asked: "What do you do to manage stress?"

He didn't say, "Do you have stress?" or "Do you feel stress?" He asked how I handled it.

I suppose that must be true of most lives: it's not *if* we have stress; it is *what we do* with it when we *do* have it.

I don't handle it.

One of my favorite biblical illustrations, which I have clung to for a decade, is that of a mother, found in the second chapter of Exodus. Jochebed, one of the Israelites (who were at the time brutally enslaved by the Egyptians), gave birth to a son. In an attempt to reduce the power of the growing Israelite population, the Pharaoh had ordered *all* male Israelite babies to be killed.

I think of this woman and her 2:18s, 3:18s, and 4:18s. Did she stay up thinking *What if?* all night? During pregnancy, did she wonder if she was carrying a boy? Had she hoped something would change—the law, the slavery, anything? Did she cry? After the birth, knowing it was a boy, did she cling to him as if every breath were his last? Did she have nightmares of the Pharaoh's soldiers coming? Did she hear phantom horses' hooves of the chariots? When did she "plan"?

Because she *did* plan. We are only given a glimpse of it in a couple verses of Exodus 2:2–3 (NIV): "When she saw that he was a fine child, she hid him for three months. But when she could hide him no longer, she got a papyrus basket for him and coated it with tar and pitch. Then she placed the child in it and put it among the reeds along the bank of the Nile."

I don't know if she was up all night thinking, but I do know that she took a basket, made it waterproof, and put her precious little bundle inside. Then, she set it in the reeds along the bank of the Nile River—crocodiles and Pharaohs and all. And she *let go*.

I guess the fact is that it wasn't *her* precious bundle. It was God's all along.

This story has played in my mind countless times.

When I have faced scary medical news, I have had to do my due diligence of preparing a basket, choosing the right doctors and the right locations, asking God to guide every step…and then I have had to let go of the basket.

When I have known a person I deeply love was dealing with intense pain, thousands of miles away, I have had to get out my pitch and tar—on my knees in prayer that God would show me my role—and then let go and let God guide the basket. Sometimes I have wished I had fishing wire attached so I could reel it back in and think on it more or do more, but don't I trust that God can guide its path perfectly?

As I watch other moms' hearts ache over their wayward adult children who just seem to go the wrong direction, I can only encourage: "You have selected the basket. You have waterproofed. You may not 'deserve' the treatment any more than Jochebed deserved to be an abused slave or to lose her son, but God does have a plan."

Of course, you know the rest of the story, right? The place where Jochebed selected to leave the basket was where the Pharaoh's daughter bathed. When she found the baby, she named him Moses, and he grew up as an Egyptian. But as an adult, through God's providential plan, he freed all the Israelites from slavery…and I could go on forever about this amazing, providential, history-making story! The implications! The impact!

The impact of one woman who made a basket…and let it go.

So how do I deal with stress? I wish it were as easily done as it is said:

Let go of the basket.

God didn't promise that motherhood would be easy, but He did promise He'd be with me every minute.

I love the old saying: "Don't worry about tomorrow; God is already there."

He's got the basket in His hands.

Love ya, girl!

Terri

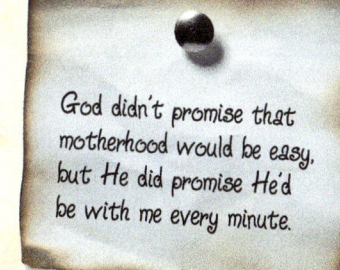

Fire! Fire! Pants on Fire!

Dear Lindsey,

A decade ago, we were excited to have moved into our new home in Grand Blanc, Michigan. Moving from a forty-year-old house to a two-year-old Parade of Homes champion was a blessing indeed. The realtor had pointed out the beautiful cathedral ceiling entryway, adorned by a chandelier of "real crystals and 14-karat-gold plating" that matched the sconces on the sidewalls. I had never owned something so "fancy." A balcony bridge on the second floor was visible just beyond, so upstairs onlookers could see people at the front door or look down to the great room on the other side. I often joked how I wished it were a drawbridge so I could put children to bed and then lift their walkway, preventing their return downstairs until I deemed it permissible.

Not long after moving in, we had a houseful of guests, some close friends and some friends-to-be, all linked by the commonality of business. I proudly took them on their requested tour of our home, pointing out the features so fresh in my mind, as taught by the realtor who had made the sale.

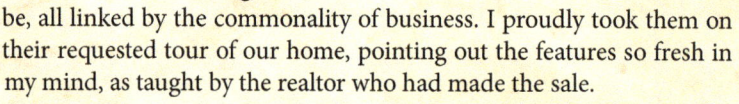

> "Mom, I know how you fly. You run down our driveway, jump and spin super fast, and then you are flying."
> —my six-year-old

As we walked across the bridge, I made my usual drawbridge joke and proceeded on to the guest suite on the other side. Suddenly, one of the guests from the back of the group said, "Uh…I think your chandelier is on fire."

I looked back to see smoke coming from the front-door side of the bridge. I quickly approached and yelled for someone on the lower level to turn off the chandelier.

The twenty people from the tour stared from the balcony; the rest gathered below because of my panicked cry. The entire party stared as the dimmed light revealed a pair of 4T underwear sparking and smoldering on one of the "real crystals" of the now unlit light fixture.

Later, when I called my four-year-old son to the scene to ask the hows and whys, he only said, "I was wondering where that went!"

I still enjoy a laugh!

Terri

If I Am to Be Queen, I Shall Be a Good One

Dear Lindsey,

In 1831 in Great Britain, a little girl was studying English history. Reading through the royal lineage, she saw her own family tree and innocently realized that she was to be the next queen. The thought overwhelmed her, and her tears drew the attention of her tutor. The little girl explained her plight, and her tutor confirmed her destiny. It was recorded that day that the young Victoria said, "If I am to be queen, I shall be a good one."[5]

Of course, Queen Victoria reigned through much of the peaceful 1800s so well that the Victorian era is renowned as a pleasant one. Furniture and architecture styles bear her name.

When talking with other wives, I am often asked questions like: "How do I get my husband to be a spiritual leader?" or "How can I motivate my husband to do more?"

> When a woman uplifts her husband, no man can knock him down. When a woman tears down her husband, no man can pick him up.

My answer is not an easy one—and I didn't like it when I first came to this conclusion:

If I want to be married to a king, I must determine to be a good queen.

Last week, I read the book of Esther. Following my pastor's series of sermons on Esther last year, it struck me how much Esther had to do to be queen! The year's worth of beauty treatments and the selection process alone are evidence of the Almighty's hand in this suspenseful, twisting, true tale of a heroine. (I highly recommend reading that little ten-chapter book of the Bible again now!) But the biggest thing in the book that struck me this time was the respect with which she treated the king.

I have been guilty in the past of looking at other women married to successful men and thinking, *Wow! It must be cool to be treated like a queen!* I can't say I ever really thought about what it would take to *behave* like one.

> My eleven-year-old: "It's annoying that boys aren't taller than girls until they're...adults... because then, they don't even care about it."

I come from the same educational background as my husband: engineering. We both had high scores on the GRE (100 percent in logic—I know...geekville), went to the same college, and had companies pay our tuition through scholarships. We went to work in the automotive industry. He worked on engine components; I worked on transmission components. And together, we made the car go.

It is a blessing when a woman can use her abilities to work outside the home, when she has her biblical priorities in line (Proverbs 31, for example)...But I hope her husband still feels like a king.

Too often, a woman will use her God-given talents to advance her family (her heart is right) but somehow end up turning her husband into a pawn instead of a king and then wonder why he won't act like a king. (Of course, I would be equally disappointed with a man treating his wife as anything less than his queen, but I digress from my point in this letter.)

Maybe there's something to this "act like a queen" stuff!

A spiritual leader will be at his best when he has spiritual followers.

I am no linguisticologist (although I can make up words!), but it seems like the word *encourage* would break down into *in* and *courage* or "to put courage into." (And *discourage* would be the opposite, or "to take courage out.") I don't know about you, but I always do more when someone is pumping courage into me. What if we pumped courage into our kings? Then we would be queens!

> "Mom! Did you see that guy's babe...or hon...or whatever you call the lady he's married to?" —J.R. (age six) while we were driving to a tee-ball game

I recently read a blog that inspired me to make my own list of ways to encourage my husband. I am sharing the first twenty, but feel free to get creative on your own.

Look out, ladies! I read this list aloud to a mixed-gender crowd of a few thousand people in Louisville, Kentucky. I was shocked by the response of the men, who shouted, "Read more! Read more!"

I guess men (like women)…and kings (like queens)…crave encouragement. Don't wait to receive in order to give it.

Make your own list—and then live it.

Determine to be a good queen.

Twenty Ways to Encourage Your Husband:

1. Enjoy a great time in the bedroom with him.
2. Send him an email that lists the A-to-Z things you love about him. (If you can't do this, it may be part of the problem. Think harder and longer; take your time…even a letter a day.)
3. Know what his dreams are, and make a scrapbook out of them for his review.
4. Ask him not what he can do for you, but what you can do for him. It is not "Do unto others only if they do unto you," but "Do unto others as you would like them to do unto you"(see Matthew 7:12 and Luke 6:31).
5. If he is concerned about eating healthy, prepare meals that align with his desires. If he would rather eat differently, treat him like an adult—an adult king.
6. Do *his* "chores" for a week, expecting nothing.
7. When he fails, forgive quickly.
8. Leave him a note in his briefcase or lunch bag, saying for example: "I am so glad to be your queen."
9. Write his goals on the bathroom mirror with dry-erase marker (if he likes your encouragement on his goals; if he likes to keep his goals to himself—let him! After all, aren't there some goals we girls like to keep to ourselves, too?).
10. Take care of yourself. Eat well, sleep well, and exercise so you are the best queen. If you can't live with yourself, it's virtually impossible for anyone else to live with you either. Self-discipline helps many more than yourself, but I could write another whole letter on that subject alone!
11. Let him be his own boss. (Too often, I am the captain of the ship when Chris travels, and it is easy to let my command-giving fall onto the king's ears when he returns—not a good method of encouragement.)
12. Initiate a great time in the bedroom.
13. Buy his favorite soda.
14. Have the kids make a "Yay, Daddy!" party complete with notes saying why they love him.
15. Talk nicely about him to others—in front of him and behind his back.
16. Be his advocate when speaking to your kids. Stand up for him, even if you need to buy time, saying for example: "I am sure Daddy didn't mean it that way. He loves you. When he gets home, you can talk to him and clear it up." How a child talks about his dad tells me a lot about his mom.

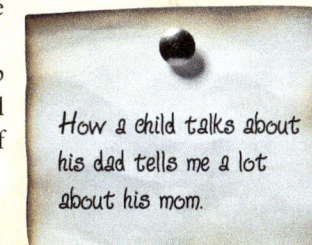

How a child talks about his dad tells me a lot about his mom.

17. Don't keep score of his hours of free time, his money spent, his reading time, etc.
18. Greet him at the door in lingerie. (First, make sure he's not bringing friends or business partners home with him that night!)
19. Protect his time. Don't invite people over or to ride to an event with you or stay with you unless he agrees. Your "followership" encourages his leadership.
20. Stop what you are doing when he comes in the door. (Don't be on the phone if you are expecting him.) Greet him as though you are happy to see him! "What you have done for the least of these, you have done unto me," said *the* King (see Matthew 25:35–40).

I can see the crown beginning to appear on your head!

In love,

Terri

Bad Queens

It is better to live on the corner of the housetop than to live in a wide house with a bad queen, to paraphrase Proverbs 25:24 and 21:9.

Dear Lindsey,

In a previous letter, "If I Am to Be Queen, I Shall Be a Good One," I talked about being a good queen (or wife), determining to be so after the story of the young future Queen Victoria. But of course, history is also filled with bad queens—as are marriages! I could not speak with such detail about such queens if I had not walked in their shoes at different times in my own marriage. Now, I see these queens walking around, torturing their miserable kings, and the country song, "Could've Been Me!" plays in my head: I know I have had moments of bad "queendom" in my life. I could've been those wives.

Four Bad Queens in Marriage:

1. Script-Writing Queen:

A script-writing queen has already plotted out how the day, her life, and even the lives of others are supposed to go. This queen is not always the star of the script; she can disguise herself as humble, as if she wants to be in the background, yet she knows everyone's lines by heart.

The worst part of the script-writing queen is that she doesn't tell anyone what the script is! She surrounds herself with eggshells, as others walk cautiously, guessing what their lines are supposed to be to make the play turn out as the bad queen intends.

The Remedy for the Script-Writing Queen:

- Stop writing scripts in your head. Discuss your expectations with those who are involved in meeting them, and then determine if the plan is agreeable.

- Give your king (husband) grace if expectations are not met. *The more you have needed forgiveness, the more you are willing to forgive.* If you have never needed forgiveness, then forgive anyway.

- Recognize God is the only scriptwriter, and live with His plan for your day. Proverbs 16:9 says, "The mind of man plans his way, But the LORD directs his steps." In other words, no matter how much planning I do, God's plan for my day will always prevail!

2. Motive-Assigning Queen:

Motive-assigning queens think they know the thoughts, desires, and intents of their kings.

When my kids were small and they fought in the car, one would often yell from the backseat, "Mom, he hit me *on purpose as hard as he could*!"

I giggle inside at the silliness of the thought, *on purpose as hard as he could*. It is as if the child had a measurement method for determining the purpose and intent of his or her sibling as well as a gauge that could decipher the magnitude of the hit in comparison to the overall ability: *on purpose as hard as he could!* Ha! But haven't I been like that with my husband?

> We asked the kids what the key to a great marriage is. My kids' answer: "Low expectations!" Ha!

> "A woman can either make a fool out of a man or a man out of a fool."
> —Chris Brady

- He left that dirty dish right in the middle of my clean sink just to see if I will clean it up.

- He is driving like Speed Racer and putting my life in danger because he thinks it's funny that it freaks me out.

- He has selective hearing and only hears what he wants to hear. He suddenly can't hear when I tell him things I need him to do.

Motive-assigning queen translation: *He didn't listen on purpose as hard as he could!* It is simply assigning a motive to his heart. *Maybe my heart is the one that needs a checkup.*

The Remedy for the Motive-Assigning Queen:

- Recognize the ailment: Anytime we catch ourselves saying, "He thinks ___," "He wants___," or "He did it because___," we are assigning motives.

- Confirm your intent analysis and strength measurement with him. In other words, ask him!

"Why are you …?" in my calm voice has often yielded answers like, "Sorry! I didn't even notice I was doing that!"—and I can thank God because he didn't even notice what I thought he was doing *"on purpose as hard as he could."*

3. Needy Queen:

The needy queen is one who depends on her husband for everything.

- She needs him to be in the kitchen, go grocery shopping with her, and notice if she changed something.

- She needs him to serve her.

- She needs him to be her source of happiness, and when he messes up, her life is messed up.

If my value comes from how my husband views me, I will be subject to his imperfect perception.

- I made his breakfast, and he didn't like it.

- I worked so hard to get the house straightened, and all he asked was why I wasn't ready for the meeting.

The Remedy for the Needy Queen:

- Do all things for the glory of God, not your own glory or even your husband's glory.

- Recognize that you are not married to a perfect person, and neither is he.

- There is only one King who is perfect, and we must be dependent on Him.

When we live a life with God as sufficient for all our needs, it is truly amazing how much better marriage can be. The weight is off of our kings' shoulders as we put all our weight on *the* King.

If I am doing all things for the glory of God (1 Corinthians 10:31), then I am not waiting with bated breath for my husband's opinion.

If I go to the car and get my own things instead of asking my husband to be my errand boy, it's amazing how many times he says, "Here, let me get that for you!"

Need God. Love your husband.

Need God. Love your husband.

4. Checkmating Queen:

Ugh.

This is the worst set of queens, and I am embarrassed to have once been a founding member. The marriage vows of the checkmating queen say, "…to have and to hold, to compete with to the death of the king or the marriage."

In Nicole Johnson's *Dropping Your Rock*, she talks about hoarding "retaliation rocks".[6] My checkmating queen picked up one rock for each mistake her husband ever made and harbored it in case of a future need to throw it at him to win a battle. Or at least she would write down his sins and mistakes to show to some counselor one day so "checkmate" can be declared as the queen wins!—and the marriage loses.

> "When you marry the right woman, you are COMPLETE. When you marry the wrong woman, you are FINISHED."
> —Samsundar Balgobin

In chess, there is a white queen and a white king. The white queen is on the same team as the white king—always. And together, they face the other side. It is *never* the white queen against the white king, as in a checkmating queen's marriage.

I don't know if it was due to having all brothers or dealing with the world-against-men attitude in the male-dominated workplace of engineering, but somewhere along the way, I began competing against my husband, instead of being on the same team. It was never a declaration or public announcement; it was more of a subtlety in the background of our marriage.

- I wanted the last word.

- I wanted the funniest joke (and, horribly, sometimes at his expense).

- I wanted to look smarter in front of friends, make more money at work, receive more awards, etc.

The Remedy for the Checkmating Queen:

- Remember, *it is you and your king against the evil forces in the world*—not *you against your king.*

- Edify one another, lifting each other up as better than yourself (Romans 12:10 and Philippians 2:3).

- *The picture you paint of your marriage in front of others (especially your children!) influences everyone around you.* If you want your son to be a king in his house one day, show him how a king is treated. If you want your daughter to have a wonderful marriage one day, then model how wonderful a marriage can be when the king and queen are on the same team—always.

The Story of the Brady Marriage…and My "Queendom"

As a newlywed, I was in a community band. I'll admit: it was an awful band; but I just wanted to keep up my saxophone playing, so I attended regularly, despite my full-time job as an automotive engineer. The night of the concert, I got dressed in formal attire, and I headed out the sliding glass back door of our basement apartment.

That's when I noticed that Chris was sitting on the couch, in his casual after-work hangout clothes.

"The concert starts at seven," I said, assuming my reminder would be enough to eject him from the couch to his closet to get dressed for the concert.

"Okay, good luck!" he said, not moving from his position.

"Well, you're coming, aren't you?" I asked, recognizing he was not.

"No, I have some things to get done" was his nonchalant reply.

My simmering mind went to a full boil. The scriptwriter within me had not allowed for him to have things on his agenda. My script for the night was for him to drive a second car (since I had already conceded that he would not want to be there an hour early for my warm-ups).

> The only difference between "marital art" and "martial art" is where the "i" is.

I stormed around getting my things and hoped my stomping would subliminally communicate my disappointment and manipulate him into coming. Words did not come out of my mouth, but smoke was leaving my ears. I was hurt. Surely he didn't love me if he thought anything was more important than seeing my concert. *He came to my concerts in college. Now he won't even come to this? Was he misleading me in college just to marry me? Yeah, that's it....He didn't love me.*

"Well, I love *you!*" I said, and I drew out the last word to be long and sarcastic, as if I were portraying how much more my love for him was than his love for me. Checkmate.

I then proceeded to slam the sliding glass door.

Have you ever tried to slam a sliding glass door?

Have you ever tried slamming a sliding glass door that desperately needs a WD-40 massage or all your might to close it one inch at a time?!

Temper makes us look so silly!

- But I was **needy**. Chris's lack of attendance was messing with my happiness that night.

- I had a **script** (that I had not printed out for him), and he wasn't following it.

- I **assigned motives**: he must not love me.

- I was **checkmating**: I definitely loved him more. I was going to show the world I was better than my couch-sitting husband, who must have tricked me into marrying him.

Ha. It makes me laugh still. That door, stuck in its tracks, ruined my dramatic departure. It screeched to a halt, and I couldn't get it to shut. I bent in my formal gown, trying to get the door to shut, so I could leave in a huff—my new script.

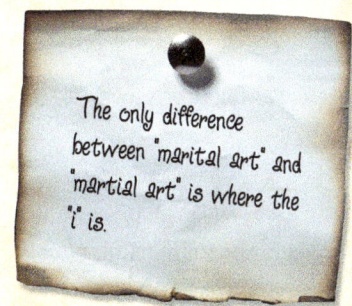

This letter could go on to many more bad queens:

- The Manipulating Queen: Close cousin to the script-writing queen, she tells half-truths or twists words to mean what she wants them to mean.

- The Victim Queen: She determines that she is a victim, and nothing is her responsibility to fix.

- The Beauty Queen: Her day revolves around her "self," and so do her priorities—spending hour after hour at the salon, the fashion boutique, the tanning parlor, and the plastic surgeon—to the point where her "self" becomes an idol of her heart.

Christian Marriage

Oh, but wait…the Good Queen exists, and with God's help, she can beat out any Bad Queen within us. (Go back and read "Twenty Ways to Encourage Your Husband" to start the process!) In chess, the queen doesn't beat the king on her own side, but she does defeat the opposing queen.

Do not grow weary, my friend. Focus on the good, and become it…*for God's glory…on purpose as hard as you can!*

In Christ,

Terri

A Stone's Throw

Dear Lindsey,

With the toddler and baby in tow, Chris and I toured our future home that was being built, while the eight- and five-year-olds waited outside in the middle of the 180-acre property. When we came outside, a newsworthy story was underway. We heard a "Bam!" and another "Bam!

Bam!" It sounded as if our car were being shot with BBs. "Bam! Bam!" Chris ran over to find our five-year-old picking up more ammo (rocks) as he proceeded to throw them directly at our Ford Excursion, five feet away.

New white scratches lined the entire right side of the black truck, and the taillight had been shattered before our arrival. "WHAT'S GOING ON HERE?!" Chris roared as he grabbed Nate's hand before the next round of pebbles could be launched.

"Crash!" we heard the glass fall from the side rearview mirror.

Bewildered, Nate replied, "I am just trying to hit the license plate."

No, I could never make these things up. Yes, my children still do things like this, and I will write about them in five or ten years—when I think they're funny.

I am a believer in giving young children grace, but this true tale from my child needed more than grace. Although unintentional, there were results that happened due to the five-year-old's actions, and those scratches, mirror, and taillight needed to be fixed. He was in trouble!

I can't tell you the number of times I was "just aiming for the license plate," and someone or something got hurt in the meantime. So often, I want to chalk it off as "not my fault," but the fact is my actions have ramifications, and I am responsible.

I regret the number of times I have put my foot in my mouth at the sacrifice of someone's heart. Instead of apologizing or clarifying, I sadly have let it go as if "It's her problem if she's going to be so sensitive" because, after all, I was only aiming for the license plate.

When I was a young filly of about twenty-three, I was 5'7" and 112 pounds, the same dimensions as a Miss America pageant contestant that year. (Okay, not the same dimensions, but the same numbers. LOL!) I wore skirts that fit and were comfortable in length to me (short!) and figured if guys looked inappropriately, that was their sin, not mine. My aim was simply to dress up and feel comfortable. However, our pastor shared a different perspective (regarding Titus 2, which tells women to be "chaste"):

"You would probably be surprised to know how many times I have had men in the church lament to me—the last guy only recently—telling me, "If only our women knew how difficult it was at times to come in here and try to focus on God while at the same time ending

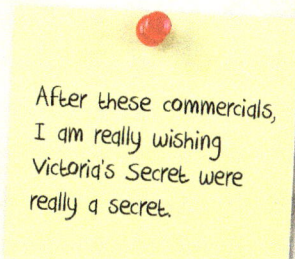

Sticky note: After these commercials, I am really wishing Victoria's Secret were really a secret.

Sticky note: If it's not my fault, that doesn't mean it's not my responsibility.

up battling my flesh over someone nearby who showed up looking like they did…the entire service became a tug of war and I have left church more defeated than when I came in."

I recognized *that* scratched paint and broken taillight I, myself, may once have caused.

You have heard that we judge others by their behavior, but we judge ourselves by our intentions. In other words, we judge others by the scratches on the truck, but we excuse (or often deny) our own scratch-making because we were "just trying to hit the license plate."

Luckily, although thrown stones indeed have consequences, there are lessons learned and paint to make things new. My son eventually paid for the damages with his labor, and he learned he needed to stop throwing stones if there was a risk of something nearby breaking.

I suppose that's the lesson: I need to stop throwing stones, since there are people all around me… breaking. I need to ask forgiveness from those whom I have "scratched" even unintentionally, so fresh paint can be applied. Of course, when we ourselves get scratched, we can remind ourselves that maybe the offender was…only aiming at the license plate.

May God bless you with intentions and actions that match.

Terri

Miscarriages and Slow Todders

Dear Lindsey,

Nate loves the verses Proverbs 3:5-6 ("Trust in the Lord with all your heart and lean not on your own understanding. In all your ways acknowledge Him and He will direct your paths."). He often cites it as the reason he was born. You see, when he was three years old, I told him of a sad day for me, when I had miscarried a baby.

I had told him, "Before you were born, I was so sad that the baby died. I didn't understand at the time of my sadness, but God had a better plan. If I had never miscarried that baby, then I would never have had *YOU*!"

I remember his eyes sparkling with delight when He realized he had such a special role in God's plan. I have heard him telling others this story with such zeal, almost evangelically, citing that verse.

On a completely different note: Years later, I had two toddlers in car seats and two older boys needing to be picked up from soccer, and I once left the house in a huge hurry. (Okay, it happened more than once, but this one I really remember!) As we pressed the speed limit down El Dorado Parkway in Cape Coral, FL, one of the toddlers complained she wasn't buckled and she "couldn't" do it! I kept encouraging her, but to no avail; I had to stop the car. Pulling off the road a mile from my house, I got out of the large truck, walked all the way around to the back right seat and buckled her before walking all the way back around to the driver's seat, and I continued down the road. *Uggh*! I thought in frustration. *Life is so SLOW at the pace of a three-year-old!*

One mile further, approaching a four-way stop, I saw a car coming from my left race through the stop sign at about sixty miles per hour and continue straight as if running from something. At that moment, I thanked God for my "slow" toddlers who had just saved us from an accident.

Who knows the number of times "angels watched over me" and I was unaware. As the Amy Grant song says, "a reckless car ran out of gas before it ran my way."[7] When we are late because we made a wrong turn or had to wait on a train, I often think of the "reckless" car I probably missed.

The problem is the "angels" are sometimes disguised as miscarriages and slow toddlers.

Because I trust God for my eternity, I can certainly trust Him with the next twenty-four hours.

Love ya!

Terri

Tea Party with a Fashionista

Dear Lindsey,

Christine's first word was, "shoe." It should have been my first indication that by age seven, she would be a *fashionista*: "A person devoted to fashion clothing, particularly unique or high fashion."[8] (I had to look it up in the "Urban Dictionary"!)

"Mom, can I *uplift* your outfit a bit?" she once asked me after seeing what I was wearing.

"Mom, why don't you wear *this*?!" she often asks while fingering through formal gowns in the back of my closet, finding it hard to believe they aren't part of my daily attire.

Salice Finds Her Style was the name of yesterday's book that she created in pencil and paper. I couldn't help but think she was third-partying me while I read it and recognized myself in her descriptions of her poor, fashion-handicapped character, Salice.

Although we know people, and especially children, spell love "T-I-M-E," author Josh McDowell says that it is not enough to spend time with our children. In order to really speak their love language, we must spend time doing what *they* love.[9] I suppose that is why my shoulder is still sore from a soccer injury I incurred almost one year ago! I was only trying to speak my son's love language by being his goalie!

I am sure McDowell's advice was still on my heart when I planned to celebrate Christine's eighth birthday last year. I know my tea-party days may be limited as her birthdays advance, so I wanted to go to a place of which I had heard: "A Southern Belle and the Yankee Tea Room" in Apex, NC. I let Chris in on the secret, so he could participate. He was all set to meet us, dressed in a suit and tie, as a surprise.

Here's where her love language came in:

"Christine, for your birthday today, you can pick whatever you want out of my closet, and I will wear it. You can do my hair and makeup—using the *real* stuff! And I will take you out for a mother-daughter shopping day and tea party."

"REALLY?!" she said with a priceless smile of adult teeth squeezed into a kid's mouth, while her freckles seemed to equally beam.

I bought her a "southern belle" costume dress and promised to do her hair and makeup as well.

After our makeover party in my bathroom that morning, we headed to downtown Apex to explore the adorable storefronts, beginning with the coffee shop for me. (Since I am not a big fan of shopping, every shopping friend of mine knows that a coffee stop will extend my shopping endurance.) Next was the used-book store, where I paused to let her read her treasures in a comfy recliner, just her size. In our formal attire, we strolled arm in arm to the décor store, My Girlfriend's Closet consignment shop, and the fancy clothing boutique and finally ended at the teashop. As we sat to place our order, a tall, dark, and handsome man walked in to top my present with a precious bow: Daddy.

We enjoyed the finger sandwiches, scones, candied nuts, and even chocolate-covered potato chips next to our cups of raspberry chocolate tea. When it was time to leave, I asked if she wanted to ride home with Daddy or me, and of course, her knight was chosen. Chris and his princess namesake walked hand in hand toward his Jeep that was parked just outside. My car, however, was a few blocks to the right, so I strolled with a smile on my face while people hustled and bustled around me, busy with their day, unaware of my extraordinary morning. I thanked God for these moments as a stay-at-home mom when we were able to create memories that will hopefully last forever, since the tea parties won't.

> My seven-year-old told me she wants to give me a manicure with her new spa kit. She has something special to push back my "tentacles."

Suddenly, I felt stares. All morning, Christine and I had been the subject of glances as people smiled approvingly at our morning out. Now, I walked alone past a restaurant with a table of ten ladies enjoying an outdoor lunch when I quickly realized the subject of their stare: *me*! I was wearing blue eye shadow up to my eyebrows, hot pink lipstick, crookedly streaked blush, and a formal teal gown with a bow draped to the ground. Alongside my daughter, I had felt like a queen to my princess, but now, I must have looked like a lady of the night making my walk of shame to my car for my morning trip home. Hee! I got the giggles as I walked, adorned in embarrassment, but I held my head high—because my dress wasn't for those ladies. It was for my princess. And she had left with my knight in shining armor in his chariot. Blessings abounded.

May God bless you with memory-making moments!

In love,

Terri

Message from the Massage: Good Luck with That!

Dear Lindsey,

While pregnant with my third child, I had "Barbie doll leg syndrome"—the term I used to describe the feeling that my leg had disengaged from my body and was only being held in place by a rubber band stretched through the socket. It was painful, almost to the point that labor sounded like a picnic. Daily life as a mother of two active boys, ages three and six, became especially difficult as I dragged my leg a foot behind (pun intended), trying not to show my limp.

> My son asked me if I know who Chuck Norris is. I told him, "No, but Chuck Norris knows who I am."

Whether motivated to get me to stop whining or just being thoughtful, my loving husband suggested I get a massage. The thought of an hour of recumbent silence sounded too good to be true.

It was. My massage therapist must have had too much coffee or simply a genuine interest in me because she was far from silent. "When are you due? Is it twins or triplets?"

That frequent question began for me shortly after the second stripe showed on the pregnancy test—when people couldn't believe my large size for just one baby. I felt as if someone had changed my name to "Dang, girl!" because that was how everyone greeted me. "Dang, girl! I thought you weren't due for months!"..."Dang, girl! What are you eating?"..."Dang, girl! How many are in there?! Are you sure they didn't make a mistake?"

A flight attendant once stopped me from getting onto a plane when I was barely halfway through my pregnancy. She was obviously nervous about my size, as if I were about to give birth. She asked, "Can you fly?"

Insulted, and without slowing my walk into the jetway, I replied, "In a plane!"

Once a male co-worker exclaimed, "Wow, you look pregnant from behind now."

"The only thing she's splitting these days is her pants!" someone humorously (yes, I thought it was funny; better to laugh than cry) answered when a waitress asked if I would be splitting my fajitas for dinner.

My kneecaps had disappeared in a pudge of fluid, not to appear again until after the birth. When I bent to tie my shoe, I would think, *What else can I do while I'm down here?*

My massage therapist continued the questions, and my dream of a silent hour vanished.

"Are you having twins?"

"No. And yes, *I am sure*."

"When are you due?"

"Four weeks."

"Are you nervous about labor?"

This was really a trick question because I *was* nervous about *one* aspect of labor: the fact that I had only felt *fifteen minutes* of contractions with my second son. He arrived after four contractions, before the ambulance arrived—actually before I had even gone down to the first floor of our house. My mother and Chris delivered Nate, although I like to say he delivered himself (at nine pounds, eight ounces!), and they caught him.

Earlier during this pregnancy, my doctor had asked a similar question: "Are you nervous about delivering at home again?"

I said, "No, I'm nervous about delivering in the grocery store!"

But in a continuing attempt to get this massage all the way to silence, I answered shortly, "No, I'm not nervous. I am actually excited to find out whether it is a boy or a girl."

"You don't know if it's a boy or a girl? Are you kidding?! Aren't you going to find out?"

"Well I hope so; I'll have to dress it" was my normal comeback to that routine question.

This caused controversy for the rest of the hour, as she questioned why I didn't find out and how I could possibly wait, knowing I already had two boys. Wasn't I dying to know if it was a girl?

The hour was over; my dream of silent relaxation was crushed. I got off the massage table, putting pressure back onto my leg joint, and my leg was still disconnected. After I paid the receptionist, my therapist popped her head into the lobby for a final good-bye. As I limped away, she yelled from behind: "Good luck with that sex!"

I quickly felt the need to interpret the statement for every stranger now watching me hobble unevenly through the waiting room, "She means gender! Gender…of the baby! I am having *one* baby in *four weeks*, and I don't know the *gender*, so she is telling me 'good luck with that *gender*'!"

My daughter was born one week later…in the hospital.

Love ya!

Terri

I had a good hair hour Monday. (Sorry if you missed it.)

"Why do they call it an Oreo bird if it's not black and white?" —my five-year-old when I told him that orioles are orange

Our third week in Italy: My five-year-old just asked me if they speak English in North Carolina.

My five-year-old said, "No, Mom, I don't want to wear long pants today…unless there's a sword fight in the front yard; then I'll change into pants."

Nate (age ten) asked with a mallet in his hand, "Is it okay to hit someone if they say it's okay?" as my five-year-old stood by him wearing a helmet.

Hard to Swallow

Dear Lindsey,

Pregnancy, although an answer to years of prayer for me, was not always the joy I thought it would be. For one of my four pregnancies, every day began with morning sickness, which never seemed to understand when noon had come and gone.

Once, while I was out at lunch with my two-year-old, the "morning" sickness hit immediately after I had eaten lunch. I quickly headed for the bathroom, where I plopped my purse and my little one on the floor as I urgently grabbed the receptacle. When I was done, I turned to my two-year-old to apologize.

He looked up at me and said, "Mom, is that baby in your belly still making you sick?"

"Yes…I guess it is," I said, wiping the sweat from my brow.

"Well, then why did you swallow it?"

Smiles,

Terri

"Mom, I failed at trying to fly."
—my five-year-old

In the ladies' room, my five-year-old son asked, "Why would anyone pay twenty-five cents for a napkin in this machine? Paper towels are free!"

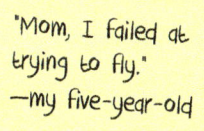

Christine (age nine): "Mom, we caught a (baby) copperhead with my butterfly net! Can you blog about it?"

"Mom, can I get my own Twitter account so I can tweet the funny things you say?"
—Christine (age nine)

Holland or Italy: Just Passing Through

Dear Lindsey,

Emily Perl Kingsley wrote an essay in 1987 called "Welcome to Holland." In the writing, she analogizes what it is like to have a special-needs child. She describes it as if you are planning a trip to Italy. While you are anxiously awaiting the cuisine, the Tuscan views, and the beautiful art, you save money, pack the bags, and buy the plane tickets. However, after the plane lands, a flight attendant announces, "Welcome to Holland." Your dreams are at first shattered—and some permanently changed, as you realize your dream of Italy is far away because now you are "stuck" in Holland. At first, maybe you can't breathe at the news, but as time passes, you soon recognize there is a lot to be thankful for in Holland, like tulips and windmills and even some art.[10]

I have nothing against Holland; I have been there briefly, and it was beautiful. However, I thought the author did a phenomenal job describing what it is like when our lives take a turn out of our control.

I keep a prayer journal, and each morning, I try to grab some quiet time with my journal, Bible, and coffee. I write down things for which I am praying, sometimes Bible verses, or processed thoughts—to keep Satan from hijacking them again. Since I am at the end of another journal, I was reviewing the pages this week to praise God for answered prayers and pray for strength to praise Him for the "unanswered" ones too (although I truly believe all prayers are answered; the answer may just be "no" or "not now" or "I have something else in mind" [Isaiah 55:8]).

As I looked over my prayer journal, I saw many "trips to Holland" in and among the prayer requests:

job loss,
family robbing family,
strained in-law relationship,
special needs of a child were more complicated than predicted,
wayward adult children, divorce,
addiction, bankruptcy, cancer,

> widowed, migraines,
> permanent injury

The above list is surely minimal compared to the private struggles people face daily.

I suppose I don't know many children who dream of having their lives diverted. We often plan, save, pack bags, and board the plane…but…

We forget Who the Pilot is.

The things I know of Holland are:

- **God is in Holland.** As cliché as it sounds, I know He is there, despite how far away we may feel (Psalm 139:7–12).

- **God planned the trip to Holland; He is the only Pilot.** You have heard, "If God is your co-pilot, swap seats." There is a purpose for every day of the life He gives, even the hardest ones, to make us who we are meant to be (Romans 5:3–5).

- **It is okay to mourn when you land in Holland.** (Blessed are those that mourn, says Matthew 5:4.) Even Christ mourned in "Holland." He went into the Garden of Gethsemane and prayed to God, "Please, if possible, don't make me go through this" (see Matthew 26:39). God had a plan—even for His own Son in "Holland." Had Christ not gone through Gethsemane and the dread, I think I would have a difficult time believing He was truly human. "Holland" made Him human. It's okay to be downright sad when life takes a turn you didn't want.

  > *I think the Lord likes keeping me "in limbo" because it is there that I seek nothing but the comfort of His arms.*

- **There are people right next to you in life who are in Holland whether you know it or not.** "Be kinder than necessary, for everyone you meet is fighting some kind of battle," said John Watson.[11] When my twenty-eight-year-old friend Diana Hummell was in the middle of her battle with liver cancer, not a soul could tell from the outside. She was as beautiful as ever. She told a story of being in the grocery store to pick up some items for the family, moving slowly after one of the surgeries. Some people in the store were so annoyed that this woman, taking so long to choose milk or pay at the checkout, was delaying their busy lives. I wept at the thought of the number of times I too had been annoyed by a slow driver or checkout attendant, not realizing their Holland status.

- **God has not given you anything He can't handle** (see Philippians 4:13). What if we put our problems into a basket and passed it around to millions of people, each relinquishing his problems into the basket? *But* the catch is that the basket will come back around, and you have to pick one of the problems out of the basket. You would want your own problem back. Why? Because God has plans for *you* (Jeremiah 29:11). He has given *you* specifically what you need to make it through. Your testimony will be a strength onto which others can hold.

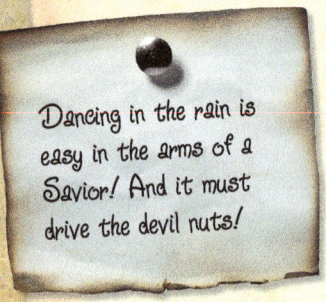

> *Dancing in the rain is easy in the arms of a Savior! And it must drive the devil nuts!*

- **There are other passengers on your plane in Holland** who will be blessed to know you. C. S. Lewis said that a friendship is born the minute someone says, "What? You too? I thought I was the only one."[12] There are people on the plane whom you never would have met unless you were there, and there is a reason your journeys have coincided.

- **There are tulips in Holland.** "I can't see tulips!" a friend of mine cried in anger after her husband's infidelity became public knowledge, opening wounds that had taken years to close in their private past. During the time of mourning, the tulips don't always show or grow. But we are called to look for tulips eventually. Gene Edwards, in his book *Exquisite Agony (Crucified by Christians)*, says that even Christ hesitated in accepting the plan by asking for the removal of the cup (Matthew 26:39), but the important part is that He peacefully accepted "Thy will be done" after the brief hesitation.[13] "In everything give thanks" (1 Thessalonians 5:18), Paul says. That doesn't mean we give thanks for the cancer, or thanks for the sin; but in my opinion, it means we seek the tulips for which we can give thanks. When a thick wall of sadness is felt on all sides, open up a journal and write down three things for which to be thankful…a sunrise, a happy memory, a God who has a plan for your eternity. The tulips are there, but some would never have been seen had we not had to dig so deeply to find them. Sometimes the tulips are disguised in "miscarriages and slow toddlers," but their beauty can be found when we dig deeply…or wait. A thankfulness journal is sure to brighten any day as it helps us refocus on sunshine.

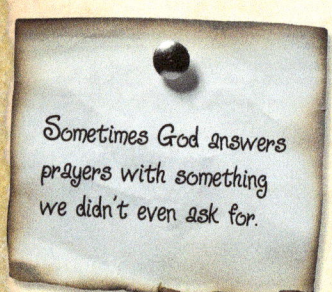

> *Sometimes God answers prayers with something we didn't even ask for.*

- **This too shall pass** (Revelation 21:4). It is often times "in Holland" that force our surrender to God's flight plan. Many believers go through a very dark hour or more, questioning God Himself, before they truly surrender and enjoy the peace that doing so provides. I drove 163 miles out of my way during one such dark time. I have heard it said that criticizing God for not solving our problems is like criticizing an author for not resolving the conflict less than halfway through the book. God's plan is bigger than yesterday, today, or this year; it's eternal.

In my husband's words, *"This probably won't be the last of your suffering, but*

your suffering won't last."

Whether we are in Holland or in Italy, the truth is we are just passing through.

Love you and praying for you,

Terri

Act like the Mom!

Dear Lindsey,

When J.R. was three, I had a terribly embarrassing night! I invited my pastor's wife and daughter over for dinner, since our husbands were traveling together. She innocently asked who would like to say the prayer, and J.R. was the first with his hand up. His prayer went like this: "Dear God, please make all these people go away so it can just be our family for dinner."

There are plenty of things my children say and do like this that are embarrassingly out of my control. But there is a completely different set of things that my children say or do that is just screaming for me to *lead*. I love it when Orrin Woodward, *New York Times* bestselling author of *LeaderShift*, talks about the moments in life when he feels something is going awry and someone needs to do something. Suddenly he thinks, *Woodward, you're the leader. Now act like it!*[14]

There are many times (a day!) that I have to remind myself of that. *Terri, you're the mom. Now act like it!*

I think I could confess for hours about this, but here are some areas where I have noticed the "terrorizing" effect of my kids and have had to scream at myself, *"Terri, you're the mom. Now act like it!"*

- *Eating.* I must admit I wonder daily if my kids will like what I am preparing for dinner. It would be so much easier to serve chicken nuggets and mac and cheese and let them deal with the habits as adults. However, when I read anything on nutrition, I realize I am responsible to God for that knowledge, and I ask myself, "*Who's the mom? Act like it!*" I know I can't force them to eat right, but I *can* limit them to snacks I approve of between meals so that they haven't filled up on empty calories of crackers and cookies by the time the meal is served. You can lead a horse to water, but you can't force him to drink—but you *can* put some salt in his oats. In essence, I can't force them to eat carrots, but I can take away the junk so they are at least hungrier when the carrots are offered.

> My six-year-old started a story tonight with, "I remember one time, before Mom made that no-sleeping-in-church rule..." Ha!

- *Restaurants.* Kids want to decide where we go. Kids want to run around. Kids want to order expensive foods, junk foods, or junk drinks. If friends are present, I feel the pressure of the terror factor even more, since I can see the habits of the friends' families in restaurants. *But… You're the mom. Now act like it*! runs through my head. If I want them to share a meal because it's economical and better quality than the kids' menu, then that's *my* choice. Teaching them to drink water at restaurants could become a lifetime habit of saved money and good nutrition. Acting with excellence in the midst of "unexcellent" people is necessary for success in any field. What a great way for them to learn that! Life lessons in price comparison are golden to their future spouses.

- *Bedtime.* The child who says, "Mom, I can see you are tired and would like some time with Dad; I'm going to go to bed early without a fuss," has never been in my house. "*You're the mom. Now act like it!*" has saved me countless hours of sleep, time to read, and time with Chris, as I get to determine bedtime and stick to it.

- *Bathroom stops.* This is a funny one to make my top list of battles, but Chris helped me see the terrorism of this in church one day. I didn't even notice that every Sunday, I was getting up in the middle of the service to take someone to the bathroom. I never got to listen, nor did those who sat near us. When I gave my wimpy excuse, "Well, he'll wet his pants," Chris practically asked me, "And who's the mom?" When we took the kids aside and told them no more potty in the middle of the church service (or for the next two hours of a road trip or during a homeschool class, for example), it's amazing how using facilities beforehand became their priority, and I got to enjoy an uninterrupted service—as did everyone sitting near us.

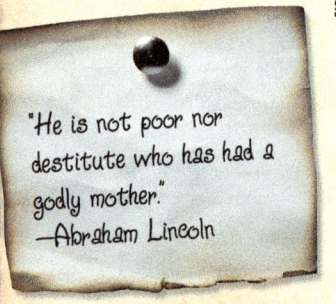

> "He is not poor nor destitute who has had a godly mother."
> —Abraham Lincoln

- *Attitude.* I witnessed a conversation between a mother and her teen the other day.

Mom: "You are taking your brother to lessons."

Teen (in a frustrated tone): "I have to do what?!"

Mom: "Try asking me that again."

Teen (still ticked): "Why do I have to take him?!"

Mom: "I need you to change your tone."

Wow! Nobody was asking who the mom was! She handled it. She didn't drop to his level and argue. She didn't even address the rebellious questions he was asking. She first got his attitude right—eyebrows up, posture straight. We are raising the next generation of adults; she's teaching him to act like one.

- *Entertainment.* I often think of a story Dr. Dobson tells in *Parenting Isn't for Cowards* about a mom who called the doctor saying her six-month-old baby was sick. When the doctor asked what the baby's temperature was, she said, "He won't let me take it."[15]

Who is that baby's mom?!

I have heard many moms say, "I can't get my kids to play outside," or "My kids won't read," or "I can't get my daughter off her screen."

> Mom, do not reward the self-centered tears of a toddler, or you will raise a self-centered adult.

Who's the mom?!

Ah, girlfriend, sometimes it just feels good to get all of that out. I *know* we are the moms, but doesn't it feel better to know that we are banded together? It's comforting to know that most kids are fighting with weapons from the same old arsenal. Unmentioned skirmishes loom: the push-back on what to wear, or personal hygiene, or the dreaded kids' chore list. The list is endless. But we know that things are less daunting when we stay the course and consistently stay the mom! Of course, in my life, prayer is at the beginning of every change. When I noticed my frustration in these areas, I thought I would share to encourage you to stay strong. I'm beside you! We can do it. *We are the moms! Let's act like it!* ☺

Love ya!

Terri

The Gift That Says, "I'm the Big One!"

Dear Lindsey,

I know it's not much to look at, perched on my office bookshelf among the cluttered books, but just seeing it floods my memory and heart, fulfilling the intention of any gift.

My husband, Chris, had taken the boys, aged two and five, to the store and handed them ten dollars each. He told them they could buy anything they wanted for me for my birthday.

Nate, full of personality (and leaving very few of his thoughts to mystery) had those pudgy cheeks the church ladies would squeeze. Always a competitor, when asked his age, he would answer, "Five," (his older brother Casey's age) with full confidence.

"My! You are such a cute little boy!" a stranger had once told him.

Nate replied, "I'm not little!…Except when I look in the mirror…Then I'm still little, but I'm not little *for real*." (But it sounded more like he said, "I'm not wittle!") Ha! Such spunk!

Casey, a sweet-spirited pensive type, made the perfect best friend of opposite personality. I am sure he kept the birthday shopping in line, as he turned down Hot Wheels and guns, aiming for the perfect gift for Mom, not himself.

The package wasn't wrapped professionally. Evidence of novice hands' work made it all the more special. Nothing needed tearing for the present to be opened, since the young deliverers who shared in handing it to me had torn most of it. They stood, or maybe bounced, in anticipation, waiting for my response to their deeply thought-out purchase.

The torn colored paper revealed the gift: two pigs.

Chris stood in the background, smiling so hard his cheeks might have cracked. It was truly delightful to see these two boys so excited to give. Casey explained the reasoning for the choice: "They are two brothers, just like Nate and me. We put our money together to buy it! We thought if you put it in your office, then you would think of us. We knew if we got you candy or something, you might eat it, and then it would be gone. But this you can keep *forever*. It says, 'I love you,' because we do!" his reasoning continued while I basked in the joy of the moment. I gave hugs of gratitude while they both beamed with pride over their selection.

Afterward, I cleaned up the papers and sent them for their pajamas to begin the bedtime routine. As Casey started toward the stairs, Nate suddenly turned away and ran to my side, cupping his mouth to my ear so Casey wouldn't hear.

"I'm the big one!" the two-year-old whispered, happily pointing to the pigs, which ironically both looked identical. That adorable memory of my "big" two-year-old sits on the shelf where the pigs still reside ten years later.

What makes the gift special?

- Chris. He thought to take time out of his busy schedule to let toddlers do the shopping.

- It's the thought that counts—always; their hearts beamed brighter than the most valuable diamond.

- The two-year-old's and five-year-old's antics are no longer in my house; I cherish those memories. No material possession could ever rank over moments that cannot be relived except in our memories. Some things truly are priceless.

Letters to Lindsey

Dear young mother: Please remember that toddlers are a gift, temporary though they are. When it seems you can't get anything done…when you have more boxes to check than checkmarks in the boxes every day…when you are exhausted with an illness and realize you still have more kids who'll get it…when you are tired of finding syrup in places you didn't know it could get to (and you haven't even had pancakes in weeks!)…stop and find a memory for which to thank God. Blow some bubbles. Drink in the smile. Pinch the cheeks. They disappear more quickly than the to-do list.

May you find the value behind the gifts you give and receive. I think the remembrance of the giver is "the big one" of them all.

In love,

Terri

My twelve-year-old just asked me what a floppy disk is.

"But it IS still shaped like a heart!" Christine said when her dad told her to put down the chewed gum she had found in the dirt.

After watching an oyster open up and reveal its pearl, my five-year-old exclaimed, "Where did he get the plastic to make it?!"

"Look, Mom! Someone tied their shoes to the telephone wires to make sure planes don't hit the wires."
—my seven-year-old

J.R. (age five) just asked me, "Mom, is this the kind of toothpaste you CAN'T eat?"

It Began as a Walk in the Park

Dear Lindsey,

Positive Influence

The seeds had been planted five years earlier, but they didn't actually begin to sprout until one day when I took a walk to the park. I was married with one child. After walking my then one-year-old to the park on a Thursday morning, I found teenagers playing on the play set. Disappointed that these "truant hooligans" were using the equipment for tag, I turned my stroller around to head home, since running teens would not make a safe environment for my newly walking little one.

That is when one of the teens yelled, "Hey, everybody! Get off the playground equipment! There's a baby here to play!"

I had somehow become accustomed to rude teenagers, who were too often self-centered (and likely skipping school), at this park. I couldn't believe my ears! One of the girls came over, looked me in the eyes with a confident smile, and said, "Here, you can have the play set; we will go over to the woods to continue our game."

> Brady homeschool survivor course: leave two kids in Greensboro, thinking they're in the other car, and have them find home. Okay, okay, we went back.

"What planet are you from?" I asked. Okay, not really, but I could have asked that because I was that surprised by their respectful behavior toward my son and me.

Not one of them was wearing something I would not wear—or something I would be embarrassed for her to wear if she sat next to my husband on a plane. I realized they might make good babysitters, so I asked them for their phone numbers. They were excitedly giving me their names when I realized *I was asking complete strangers to babysit my kid!*

I decided I needed references—which was when I asked what school they attended and found out they were homeschooled. For the first time, I thought, *These homeschoolers are different, and if this is the fruit of the homeschool tree, maybe I should stop judging them and investigate how those roots began!*

I had never heard of homeschooling until I was an adult. Chris and I had gone to public school, and no other path for my children had ever crossed my mind. The first I heard of homeschooling was as a newlywed when I attended a family funeral. There I met Chris's cousins, who homeschooled. *That is bizarre!* was my only thought.

> My seven-year-old: "Dad, I ate a lot, but more just kept magically appearing!"

It is sad, but my first look at almost any change is always a negative look, with my mind locked shut.

The family almost whispered about those cousins, as if they agreed with my "bizarre" label. My judging response was mostly in the form of questions that I didn't have the courage to ask…because I wasn't seeking answers, only judging:

- Isn't that against the law?
- Do they think they are better than the mass public, so their children need different teaching?
- Do they know they can't shelter their kids forever (assuming that is what they are trying to do) and those kids are going to have to face the real world one day?
- I hope they know what they are doing; lives of children are at stake!

But seeds were planted, and they grew in God's timing—which happened to be five years later, when I took the walk to the park.

Negative Influence

> I took the kids to the North Carolina Art Museum today! We saw paintings called "DO NOT TOUCH" and a statue called "DO NOT CLIMB" (according to them).

Fast forward from my park story two years, and I had a three-year-old and a baby.

My neighbor two doors down in that park's neighborhood also had a three-year-old within a couple months of Casey's age. She and I were very different. While my husband and I worked on beginning a business of striving for excellence in life and attended church regularly, she and her husband headed in a different direction. I devoured Dr. Dobson's parenting books, chose to avoid allowing our children to watch TV or movies, and endeavored to improve myself with the same disciplines. She had favorite soap operas, used R-rated language in normal conversation with her children or me, and often referred to her husband as the bleeping so-and-so who wouldn't clean the toilet! The f-word was her favorite descriptor; her husband was considered her servant and her children her burden to bear if they ever stepped away from the television. I will never forget the chill that ran down my back the day she excitedly told me, "Our boys will be able to walk to school together!"

I have heard that we are a product of the books we read, the words we hear, and the people with whom we associate. I suddenly realized that although, as an adult, I can choose my books, audio recordings and surrounding people, my someday five-year-old would not have that option. He would be a product of his zip code, which determined the school he would attend.

Around this same time, a good friend of mine innocently shared a story of her first-grader.

She had gone to school to help with the class and took pity on her son's classmate, a six-year-old who was working through his lettering book. While the rest of the class used the "writing station time" to go through one letter at a time and had mostly progressed to the "R-S-T-U-V" stage, this little guy was still on the "D-E-F-G" pages. She knelt down and helped him, while he got more and more frustrated.

The teacher ran over to my friend and told her to stop helping the boy. The teacher then turned to the almost tearful boy and gave him a verbal lashing for being so slow and behind the class, and he would surely be doing letters in summer school if he didn't pick up his pace! My friend was upset, seeing the damage the teacher's words could do to the boy but not sure what to do about the situation. Obviously, there may have been much behavioral history with that child in that class, but the teacher's lashing threats didn't seem likely to inspire improvement. Besides, there were twenty-five other students that needed the teacher's attention; she certainly didn't have time to cater to every rabbit and snail, so she was choosing. I might have done the same if I were a teacher of twenty-five six-year-olds!

It was around this time that it dawned on me: If I were hiring someone to watch over my children thirty hours a week, it would not be a light decision. I would be interested in the person's love for children, patience and understanding during challenges, religious stance, interest in flying planes into buildings, and the many other rights and wrongs on which people in our country agree to disagree. I believe we should take the same approach to "hiring" someone to be with our children (plus twenty to thirty others in the classroom) for thirty hours a week. Even if *many* kindergarten teachers could teach my children better than I or have more patience, more experience, and more creativity than I, *not one* could love them more than I. Therefore, we chose to homeschool…at least for a while.

> While playing Bible Blurt with my seven- and five-year-olds, the definition given was "the present day." Both blurted out simultaneously, "BIRTHDAY!" (The answer was "today.")

Define what you want. Learn from somebody who has it. And do what he or she has done.

I hunted down the mother of those teens from the park two years prior. I was sure she thought I was crazy (since my oldest child was three, I was hardly putting him in school yet!), but I liked the fruit shown in her girls that day, and I wanted my children to display it. I wrote down a list of questions and invited this otherwise stranger to lunch so I could grill her on them. I saved the list, and recently, I came across it. (The list and her answers are attached at the bottom of this letter.)

As with major decisions, Chris and I prayed while we listed the pros and cons of each schooling scenario and then made the decision that was best for the Brady family. My goal with these letters on homeschooling is not to make my decision be your decision but to encourage you to strive for excellence even in educating your children. I am embarrassed to say that there was a time when I didn't believe that my children's education fell within my responsibility.

"Isn't that part of paying taxes?"

Now I think differently.

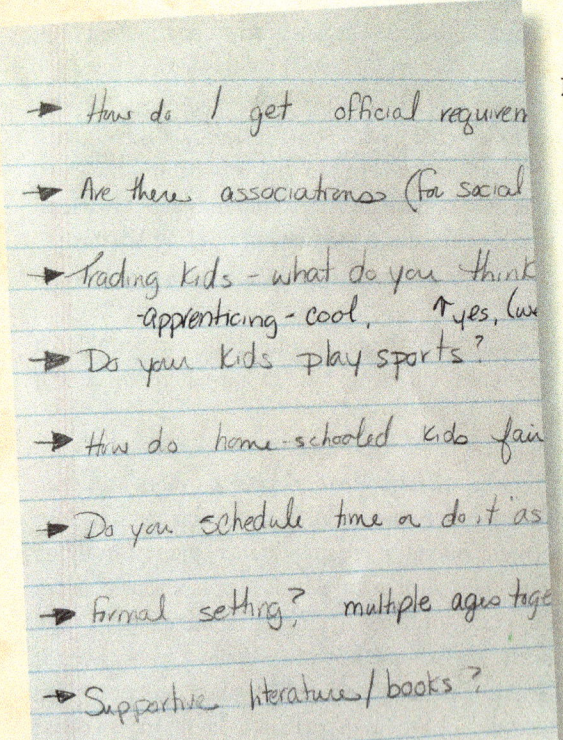

Homeschooling

I have been very impressed with the homeschoolers I have met and would love them to influence my children. When I hear my daughter say, "Mom, can you wake me up at 6:00 a.m. tomorrow so I can read before school?" or a young man at church announce, "I am selling my ski-boat that I bought when I was thirteen with money from the business I started" (selling audio recordings of his piano playing), I recognize fruit on a homeschooling tree. Homeschoolers do not go without criticism, though; I have met many who are too shy, some who seem non-perseverant, and a friend this week told me she knew a family of them that was "rude, just rude!" But in my humble experience, the odds are that the fruit is the kind of sweet that I want to experience in my home.

I am sure that God will continue to write a testimony for each of us. Now, with two kids in school and two in homeschool, I have been able to reflect on the pluses and minuses enough that I thought they were worthy of sharing in the next few letters. Whether you homeschool, public school, or private school, the principles and suggested reading material apply.

In love,

Terri

My five-year-old: "If adults say it's a short wait, that means it's a really, really, really long time!"

My Original Questions I Asked the "Stranger" Homeschool Mom of the Kids from the Park:

Q. How do I get official requirements?
A. Go to www.hslda.com and look it up by state.

Q. Are there associations (for social interactions, etc.)?
A. Yes. Search for the nearest homeschool store, and they normally have a list.

Q. Trading kids for certain subjects: what do you think?
A. We have not done it often, but it is helpful in higher math classes or for foreign language if you don't have the experience. Also, we have found that apprenticeships are the best training there is, so we often trade kids to apprentice in new skills at our businesses.

Q. What about sports?
A. In Michigan [where I lived at the time], it is the school's option to include or not include homeschoolers. [Since then, Tim Tebow has made homeschoolers in sports a little more visible because in Florida, they are allowed to play on school teams. It varies by state, but many competitive sports (gymnastics, travel soccer, and baseball) outside school are even more competitive than the school sports.]

Q. What about socialization?
A. Socialization doesn't occur with kids; peer pressure does. Social skills come from parents. [As comedian Tim Hawkins likes to say, "Why does everyone think kids should go to school to get socialization? That's where they get in trouble for socializing!"]

Q. How do homeschooled kids fare in college?

A. They do as well as public school kids. [That was her answer in 2002. My research as my oldest entered high school shows that colleges include homeschoolers as a normal part of their admissions. They have pages dedicated to homeschooler requirements for admissions. Also, some states (at least Florida and North Carolina) have a "free college" program that begins at age sixteen, where academically gifted students can take college courses at the local college and actually earn an associate degree as they graduate from homeschool high school.]

Q. Do you schedule time or do it "as you go"?
A. We do better with a scheduled start time, but many are more flexible than I.

Q. Do you have a formal setting for school? Chalkboard? Multiple ages together?
A. It is as formal as you like. Subjects like history, where it doesn't matter the order in which you learn it, we all are together. Subjects like math, I do each child individually. I used to think I needed a chalkboard, since that is what I was used to growing up, but I found it unnecessary; it is more intimate on paper together.

Q. Gym class? Art? I don't want to limit my son to my ability.
A. Oh yes! There are plenty of classes available, so you are never limited by only your ability.

Q. I am all for a biblical foundation, but am I limiting witnessing to other people who don't have that opportunity if I don't put him in a school with them?
A. By homeschooling, you create a foundation that will be strong for witnessing. If God calls you to homeschooling, then He has other plans for when your kids will be witnessing.

Another Wise Mom, Sue Gray, Taught Me Her Principles for Homeschool:

F – Fear God, not man.

A – Acknowledge where strength comes from.

C – Conform to Christ, not culture.

E – Endure all things because Christ did first.

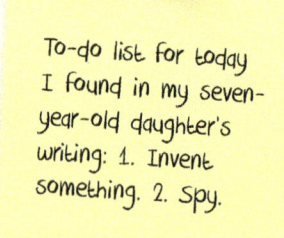

To-do list for today I found in my seven-year-old daughter's writing: 1. Invent something. 2. Spy.

Throwing Myself under the (School) Bus

Dear Lindsey,

Here are some of the most entertaining responses I have received when I said I homeschooled:

- "And you still have your hair?! That is amazing!" (Thanks, Melinda!)
- "If I homeschooled, all that my kids would know how to do is shop at Target!" (Thanks for not homeschooling, my friend!)
- "I could never spend that much time with my kids; [and even worse,] they would never want to spend that much time with me!" (Thanks, lady at the park.)

Many feel compelled to tell me why they don't homeschool—which really isn't necessary: I know it's not for everyone. I am not a homeschool Nazi who thinks there is only one way to do well for your children. I have no vendetta against public school; I love all my friends who send their kids to school; and I pretty much adore most of the teachers I have met.

More and more often, I hear, "How do you do that?" or "I wish I had done that." And my favorite response: "Can you tell me why you would do that?" (Thank you, drugstore employee!)

> My six-year-old: "Wouldn't it be cool to be a time machine guy? When you have a really good day, you could just go back and do it again."

Children Who...

Chris explained to me one day, "I don't look at our children as clay that we should mold but as seeds God entrusted to us, and we should provide the best garden for their growth."

The educational methods we have chosen are purposeful to allow our four children to grow to be adults who will:

- Glorify the Lord
- Reach their fullest potential
- Be hardworking (Proverbs 13:4)
- Have a good attitude, showing the fruit of the Spirit (Galatians 5:22–23)
- Be leaders in their homes, churches, communities, and country

In summary, the principles we would like to instill would raise happy, healthy, productive Christian Americans. There are more ways than one for that to be accomplished.

The Princess Bride Story (Sort of)

Have you heard this story about a princess? She was of marrying age, so her father began his search for the right man to whom he would promise his daughter's hand in marriage. Man after man lined up, trying to impress the king to win his favor and take his daughter's hand. A chariot race was arranged on the dirt path at the edge of the mountain, and the husband wannabes prepared their horses and carriages for the show. One man stepped forward to gain the king's attention and said, "I would like your daughter to ride with me; I will get her within one foot of the cliff's edge and bring her safely to the end of the race."

The next man could not be outdone, so he had a different promise: "Sir, I would love to win your favor so much that I will get your daughter within *one inch* of the cliff's edge and bring her safely to the race's end."

The third man walked slowly toward the king. He meekly began, "Sir, your daughter is of such value; I would not risk getting her anywhere near the edge of the cliff. I will deliver her safely, in the right time, as far from the cliff's edge as I can."

The king cancelled the race and promised the daughter's hand to the third suitor, the one who promised her safety.[16]

> *I just bought a sixteen-month calendar. Now I am looking for a twenty-seven-hour day planner.*

Why Homeschool?

I suppose I feel as if a King has entrusted four children to me, and I want to deliver them back to Him as safely as I am able. That is not to say that someone who does not homeschool is sending children over the edge of some cliff! Hear me out: I have met *many* public school-educated people who are far from the edge of any cliffs (including my perfect husband and perfect me!).

Stephen Davey, pastor of The Shepherd's Church in Cary, NC, says it this way: "I can say that we have tried all kinds of schooling for our four kids: public school, private school, and homeschool, and none of them works!"

Principal's Principles

> "Methods are many.
> Principles are few.
> Methods always change.
> Principles never do."

Homeschooling is not a principle in the Brady house; it is a method. This may be obvious since we currently have two in school and two schooling at home. This school year of fifty/fifty has shed light on both sides of the schooling methods and spurred me to write you.

I have heard that data shows that the factor most influential over a child's education is the parents' active involvement in the education—whichever method is chosen.

J.R. (age six) asked after seeing his friend's cast on her broken arm, "How did her arm fall off anyway?"

"The philosophy of the school room in one generation will be the philosophy of government in the next," Abraham Lincoln said.[17] If that statement is true, then we parents had better know and heartily agree with the philosophy of whatever schoolroom in which our children spend their weeks.

Normally, I would put a list of "recommended reading" at the end of a letter, but the recommended reading here is practically more important than this letter! So I want to include it here. Whether you homeschool, public school, or private school, these books should be required reading for any parent:

Recommended Reading:

Thomas Jefferson Education (and its sequels) by Oliver DeMille.[18] I cannot quote DeMille enough in this letter regarding school choice. I just want to print the whole book, which ironically I didn't find until I had been homeschooling for seven years! But even if you do not have children of school age, this book is an inspiration for any of us to never stop learning! (It is a great precursor to another of his books, *LeaderShift*, co-written with Orrin Woodward.[19])

The Ultimate Guide to Homeschooling by Debra Bell.[20] A must-read for parents of school-age kids. Read the first few chapters and her great school debate. If you are not choosing to homeschool, skip the rest of the book. The first few chapters provide good insight and conviction, as well as a balanced look at school choices. The back of the book has many, many options of how-tos that show the vast range of types of homeschooling.

Right-Brained Children in a Left-Brained World by Freed and Parsons.[21] ADHD is a growing diagnosis among school-aged children. This book (by someone who is not pro-homeschool) not only helped free some thoughts regarding that diagnosis (and some other options besides medication) but also shed light on some of my own weaknesses. I was amazed at how my kids fell in line with his test. He helped me find strengths in them I didn't know they had. It changed everything for one of my children because I deal with him differently in all areas, and for us, it works!

> I told the kids that the puppy broke a claw on the rough terrain. J.R. (age six) asked, "When was she on a train?!"

The Reasons We Homeschool:

In her book, Debra Bell recommends writing down *why* you homeschool. (And I would recommend writing down *what you want at the other end of school*, whichever method of schooling you choose—to keep yourself accountable to your principles.) This list has kept me "in" many times when the "bad wolf" was whispering contrary thoughts in my head; but it has also guided many decisions of ours: "Should we hire a teacher?" "Should we participate in a homeschool group?" "Should I offer to teach other like-minded families in a group or start our own school?" to name a few. We just look at how those decisions affect (or don't affect) this list of benefits and then decide.

This list will be different for all families. Just because some of these are available to homeschoolers does *not* mean that these benefits are not available through public school or private school.

Brady Family Goals and Benefits of Homeschooling:

1. *Biblical values being taught and "caught"* consistently without wavering based on denominations, legalism, or tolerance. This includes consistent discipline—not six hours of one way and then a totally different magnitude when school is out.
2. *Closely knit family relationships*: No age-group segregation to foster disunity within the family. Friends of all ages.
3. *Flexible schedule* for travel, neighbors in need, and visitors.
4. *Speed of learning catered to individual and/or subject*. Teach at a first-grade level in reading, but third-grade in math, for example.

5. *Style of learning catered to the individual.* Spoon-feeding methods and memorization versus self-teaching and reading classics; audio versus visual versus kinesthetic learning methods, etc.
6. *Avoid negative comparison or labeling* by people who don't necessarily have my kids' best interest in mind or don't love them the way I do.
7. *Avoid unnecessary negative influence* of peers, teachers, or bullies.
8. *Subjects of* my *choice, based on my priorities:* for example, Bible; Employment, Self-Employment, Business Ownership, and Investment Cashflow Quadrants (by Kiyosaki)[22]; Outdoor Play; Music Lessons; Languages; People Skills; etc.

    Once they have learned to read, they should be able to read to learn in any subject, so they can use that skill to be lifelong learners.
9. *Emphasize learning and mastery,* not grades, standardized tests, or brownie points.

    Focus on learning to think, not learning what to think (DeMille).
10. *Be influenced by other admirable homeschoolers.*
11. *Learn through experience.* Learn history through traveling with Chris, etc. I will know what they have learned, so when we travel (even to the grocery store!), I will be able to point out what applies to them at their level.

FAQs of Homeschooling:

1. Is it legal?
    a. Yes! Unless the government says our children are not our own...which unfortunately seems to be too common a trend in what I see. Go to the Homeschool Legal Defense Association website to see legal requirements for your state: www.hslda.org.
2. What about socialization?
    a. Yep. Schools are better at teaching *socialism*. Ha-ha!
    b. I asked this question about socialization originally of a homeschool mother, and she said, "Do you want your five-year-old to learn social skills from another five-year-old or an adult?" Good point.
    c. When I began, I coerced three or four good friends to do it with me. (Okay, they say I dragged them into it—but over a decade later, they have helped guide me as much or more than any opposite force.) There was no "trend" of friends to follow, but homeschoolers had laid a path that we found with ease. We got our kids together once a week for gym, music, and art. The group grew to be forty or more families with more than 100 kids by the time I left Michigan two years ago. Now here in Raleigh, North Carolina, there are thousands in the homeschool groups and several from which to choose.

> Christine (age eight) found a penny and said, "Mom, let's drop it somewhere so someone can have luck all day." I love her selfless heart!

Socialization is with the right people during socialization time; learning takes place one on one in a quiet (well, relatively quiet) home.
3. Am I able to do it?
   a. Did you teach your child to use the bathroom? Tie his shoes? Make his bed? You have been homeschooling all along.
   b. If you don't know where to begin, there are many resources available for telling you word for word what to do and say daily.
   c. In my experience, five- and six-year-olds practically teach themselves when we offer them the right educational options of reading and play.
4. What about special needs? ADHD?
   a. Special needs do not disqualify the ability to homeschool. Part of the confidence I had when I began homeschooling was due to working one on one with an autistic child, to whom his mother and I (among others) taught lessons each day, recording progress in a notebook. Thanks to God and the behavioral therapy, the non-speaking three-year-old became an active kindergartener in public school just two years later, with no diagnosis of autism present. (Read *Let Me Hear Your Voice* by Catherine Maurice[23] for additional information.)
   b. ADHD children might fare well when treated individually, at their own pace and in a well-designed environment.
5. What does it cost?
   a. A part of me wants to answer, "Everything!" since every part of me becomes part of homeschooling. But in dollar terms, the cost varies based on the method chosen, which means it varies *a lot!* Robinsoncurriculum.com offers a K–12 classics curriculum you can print from their website (or find on eBay). Amblesideonline.org offers completely free downloads and reading lists by grade level for all-library homeschooling. A local homeschool group offers classes for most high school courses in small groups for a price. Classical Conversations meets once per week with a paid teacher and then studies independently the rest of the time. As you can see, the cost varies as greatly as the method.
6. How much time does it take every day?
   a. Oliver DeMille, in *Thomas Jefferson Education*, suggests spending five hours a day doing something academic. Some kids will drive themselves more from there. Younger kids, less.
   b. In the early years (K–3rd grade), I rarely spend more than two hours working with the student. Often, after a twenty-minute reading lesson and a little math, they are off on their own—reading, exploring the outdoors, etc. Last I checked, kindergarten is still optional in many states, as well as the Brady home. The "incidental learning" through influence of reading aloud and playing games satisfied kindergarten "requirements" by age three or four for all four of our children, so I was never too worried about officially "starting school."

c. It is impossible to measure length of time in homeschooling. Maybe we work 8:00–11:00 a.m. specifically teaching, but then I see Christine (age nine) off in the woods in the backyard, carrying a journal and the *Nature Handbook* with her. And I see J.R. (age seven) trying to get his remote control car to balance, holding the magazine that he made by hand for a friend down the street. Then we snuggle with popcorn and books (see the letter: "Raising Readers") or get out the map at night, to see where Pagoo went on his journey during bedtime reading. How much time did it take to "do school"?

7. What curriculum do you use?
   a. I highly recommend anyone trying to choose a curriculum to read the DeMille and Bell books (above) before choosing. I don't use the same curriculum for all my children (see "Brady Family Goals and Benefits of Homeschooling" #5 above).
   b. When I first began homeschooling, I simply brought school home; I even boasted, "I use the same curriculum as some schools." However, experience has told me that I was not satisfying #4, 5, 8, or 10 of my reasons by just selecting a box curriculum (like A Beka or Bob Jones) and staying with it. So I branched out. I got rid of the "chalkboard mentality paradigm" I had from growing up in school. Now, we do Bible, math, and grammar/penmanship together and then focus on reading classics. (Incidentally, if anyone asks, I highly recommend to anyone starting homeschool—especially with a child who has been in public or private school—that they begin with a box curriculum like A Beka or Bob Jones because it helps you get the daily routine right before you start picking and choosing creatively.)

8. Is there an age when you shouldn't homeschool anymore?
   a. My first "age" goal to reach for each child was ten years old. The goal was that after age ten, we could reevaluate whether homeschool was right for us. Dr. James Dobson says that if a child is given one standard consistently until the age of eight to ten years old, he is much less likely to veer from it. This goes along with the fact that most discipline for obedience within a home is heavily required until around age six to ten. If, however, the foundation has many "blows to its base," when a first-grade teacher teaches evolution, for example, or promotes divorce, or doesn't punish for a child's lie, the child is more likely to question not only his beliefs but his parents' as well. So it was my first goal to get to age ten. Of course, we loved it and went beyond.

> My five-year-old just told me he is wearing three shirts today just to get his pants to stay up.

> Tonight at bedtime, J.R. (age five) asked, "Is it scratch-backing time now?"

b. My friend Donna Ascol, who has graduated four homeschoolers with high school diplomas and associate degrees at the same time and still homeschools two more, says, "If I could only homeschool two years of their whole lives, it would be sixth and seventh grade." I agree that those two years can be painfully unforgettable and unrealistic on the social skills of peers; I have not been put inside a locker since seventh grade.

c. We put our eldest in school at ninth grade, but I do *not* say that high school is the age where all should go to public or private school—if they go at all! It was right for him, but it may not be right for everyone. My second son will be coming back home for eighth grade next year: his request; our choice.

d. It goes back to praying through the pros and cons of your personal situation for each child. Reevaluating every year takes the pressure off. "No" for now doesn't mean you can't change your mind next year. Chris and I have often come to lean in a certain direction just because it has less chance of regret. I will never regret the extra time I have spent with my kids—never.

9. What obstacles are there to overcome? (The way to overcome any obstacle is to make sure the dream is bigger than the obstacle. Stay focused on your *reasons for homeschooling* anytime one of these obstacles arises in your mind. Believe me, those school buses never look so appealing to me as they do every February; I get my list of *why* back out and read it!)

   a. *Family and Friends:* With any good decision comes resistance. Well-meaning family and friends can weigh a homeschooler down. I had to understand that even though it was *truly* not in my heart, my homeschooling implied that their schooling choice was not as good as my own. Not true, but I am guessing they felt it regardless. Time allowed us all to encourage each other in our choices, knowing God has a plan for each.

   b. *Parenting:* The fluency of homeschooling is limited by our own discipline within the home. Many have told me they want to homeschool, but their kids won't listen to them. That's a sad excuse. If we can't train them to listen to us, the parents, what authority *will* they listen to? Look at statistics of peer pressure, and you get the answer. It is okay to make demands of your children—even in schooling. I am ashamed that I used to think that was "someone else's job."

   c. *Toddlers:* I don't like calling children "obstacles," but toddlers bring a challenge to homeschooling—not an impossibility, but a challenge. You can do it anyway! Yes, it is easier now that I don't have to try to dance with Cheerios in my hair to distract the one-year-old and clean up the Play-Doh of the three-year-old while teaching the six-year-old addition and the nine-year-old science, but it was all worth it. Much has been written about homeschooling with toddlers in the room, so I won't bore you with details, but I encourage you to look into it. (*Help for the Harried Homeschooler*[24] is a good place to start.) It makes me oh so sad when I hear of a mom who gives up homeschooling her six-year-old because she is afraid her three- and one-year-olds are too much of a distraction! (See the answer to #6 above for how much time it takes. Also see Obstacle #9d below [perfectionism], and overcome it. Then reread your reasons to homeschool before you consider putting a six-year-old in school due to younger siblings.)

    d. *Perfectionism:* My desire for perfection was such an obstacle that it was the most common whisper/shout in my ear trying to persuade me to put my kids in school. Sometimes the house fell apart. (*That* is funny that I just used past tense, since it *still* falls apart!) The school day almost *never* looks perfect. (*Almost* is optional in that sentence.) I too often imagined that some teacher, any teacher, would *do* a better job than I was doing. *She* would be more organized. *He* would check off every box for the day. But raising a child is not about collecting checkmarks! Raising the next generation of leaders will not always look organized! Now that I have some years of experience in homeschooling, I can confidently tell you that years of imperfect homeschooling are leading to mature children who are progressing in the direction of happy, healthy, productive Christian Americans.

Who should NOT homeschool?

1. If the only reason you want to take your kids out of school is so they don't wake you up in the morning, please don't.
2. If you are only half-interested in it, please don't.
3. If you are only mad at a teacher, please don't. Rectify things with the teacher, and then make a decision through prayer.
4. If you call your husband a "bleeping so-and-so who won't clean the toilets!" your kids could use a better influence. (Ha-ha! Remember from my last letter, "It Began as a Walk in the Park"?)
5. If you don't feel called to homeschool, nothing is wrong with you. There are other options, and God may be using your life and your children's in those situations for His glory! Press on!

In love,

Terri

> When I say good-bye to my son (age five), I kiss his hand and give a lipstick mark. Today my lipstick was light-colored; he told me, "You need more ink!"

Homeschooling Missing Ingredients (Mistakes I've Made)

Dear Lindsey,

The coupons began as a spontaneous purchase at Walgreens, although I haven't seen them there lately, so we have made our own. One coupon says, "Your choice of restaurant the next time we eat out." Another says, "Multiply your snacks by two today," and a very memorable one says, "You make the snack, whatever you want, and Mom has to eat a bite."

Hmm. Why do I do these things? I was nervous when they decided to redeem that coupon!

Fortunately, my children were nice (nicer than I probably would have been to my own mom when I was their age!) and decided that they would try to make peanut butter icing, knowing my love for peanut butter. The problem was that this six- and seven-year-old could not find a recipe, so they just guessed. They were so excited working together. I walked through the kitchen and saw my Kitchen Aid mixer on the counter as if this were a professional production. I tried to stay out of sight, but I enjoyed their whispers from a distance.

"No, no, no! I don't think there's baking powder in frosting!" I heard J.R. say. "I'm pretty sure there's vanilla, though."

"It looks like peanut butter mush!" they cackled and then hushed each other so I wouldn't hear their surprise.

"Mmm, it's good mush," Christine said, and I pictured her eyes sparkling as she took her taste-test finger out of her mouth.

"What's that white stuff in frosting?" she asked. "I think that's what's missing."

"Oh yeah! Shortening!" he yelled, and I heard his motions climbing the counter to get to the cupboard behind the prep sink.

I cringed from my office, wondering what kind of sick mind I'd had the day I thought that coupon was a good one to offer. Why didn't I say *Dad* had to taste it?

"Oh, Mommmmy!" they sang in a doorbell-toned duet. "It's ready for you to taste!" And the giggles filled the room.

I rounded the corner to see the powdered sugar box empty, with clear handprints in its dust all over the island. Measuring spoons were out, though I wondered what they had measured, since they didn't have a recipe. I did not see reptiles or worms present, so I thought it must be safe for eating. With all the courage I could muster, I took the spatula preloaded with peanut butter icing from J.R.'s hand and took a lick.

"Not bad!" I said, and they squealed with pride.

So cute!

I happened to have some ooey-gooey chocolate cookies left over from Christmas in the freezer, so we thawed them and sandwiched the icing between two cookies. Delicious! Really!

When I began homeschooling, I think I wanted a recipe to follow, but yet I *loved* being able to cater the learning to each individual child! I went with what I knew and then added some things and subtracted some things. And I still do today! But just like in Christine's and J.R.'s

> My seven-year-old said: "Yay! We're having gorilla cheese sandwiches!" This explains a lot to me about her spelling lessons.

> Nate (age eleven): "Mom, I don't need your help tomorrow. I taught myself today. I learned receptacles. The receptacle of 3 is 1/3."

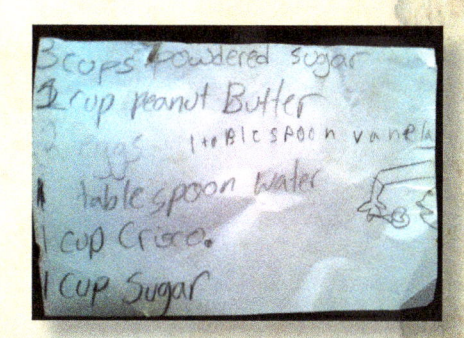

recipe, there are certain things I want to keep out. (By the way, that's their invented recipe in the photo! Use with caution!)

Some Homeschooling Mistakes Along the Way

Although I love lists, this one is not my favorite: my list of mistakes. (And it is longer than could be captured on paper and still growing!) However, I am grateful I learned from some of these… at least once so far, anyway.

1. *Bringing school home:* When I admitted to a dear friend, Sham, that I never felt like I was completing a school day right, she said sweetly, "It sounds like maybe you are bringing school home instead of homeschooling." I immediately knew what she meant, and I was guilty as charged! I had a chalkboard on the wall and even had a 1950s school desk that I found at a garage sale! I was "Teacher" during school hours and "Mom" sometime later. School wasn't done until that little book said it was done. Missing ingredient: home.
2. *Routine rut:* Routine is great! We start at the same time (approximately) each day. We do subjects in the same order (although for the first year, I wrote the subjects down on popsicle sticks and allowed him to rearrange the sticks daily). But routine can lead to ruts of "unfun" hours on end. Too often, I have become a slave master, cracking a whip, worried about the time and when summer break (for me!) would begin. I had an agenda, and it needed to be met. Similar to "putting the home in school," I realized I needed to flex. We made family sandwiches (with Mom on the bottom, of course; thanks, Marcia Robinson, for that idea), learned multiplication of 7s using football guys, added recess, put in a field trip or special lecture series by Dad (since he is at home during the day), and my older two keep telling my younger two that we used to have a "math substitute" once a week. (Shhh. Those two are doing fine with math every day!) Missing ingredient: laughter.
3. *Keeping up with Joneses:* We know that comparison is the root of unhappiness, and I really didn't think I could be that way. I mean, my kids are the best kids on earth, so how could comparing with any others ever lead to unhappiness? Well, when someone says, "We accidentally hit an opossum in our car last night, so we decided to scoop it up and take it home for science dissection," I realized, *I am completely unworthy to ever be called a homeschool mom.* (Thanks, Wendy Lukonen, my hero!) "Keeping up with the Joneses" does two things: First, it makes me feel as if I should be doing something different in homeschooling. Second, any moment I spend thinking about "what I should have done" takes away time that I could be encouraging another precious homeschool mom for doing a great job. I decided that Mrs. Jones was chosen to homeschool *her* kids. I am called to homeschool *mine*; no comparison allowed. Missing ingredient: contentment.

4. *Low expectations for my kids:* I watched Casey's math test "grades" dwindle. I was never much for keeping grades. Grades seemed to be for communicating between teacher and parents how well a student was performing. I never bothered. Instead, I looked for mastery. If he missed problems, he had to redo them until he could do them well. Red pen? Optional. One day, I realized Casey was not getting 100 percent of his problems correct—ever. Knowing my kid, I realized he was capable and completely unmotivated. Why would he care? I had no expectation for him to meet. The above "coupon" program was instituted to encourage 100 percent on the first try of a math assessment (test). It was amazing how as soon as there was incentive, he checked and double-checked his work before turning it in. He had never known that I expected 100 percent because I had communicated otherwise. I soon recognized other areas of my low expectations: excellence of chores, cleanliness of rooms, good attitude, edification of siblings, etc. Ugh! Writing this reminds me of how much I still need to do! Missing ingredient: great expectations.

5. *Too many activities:* When opportunity knocks, that doesn't mean we have to answer. We could go to a co-op all day on Thursdays, play homeschool soccer on Friday mornings, and go to homeschool art class on Monday afternoons. And don't forget library story hour next door—it's so convenient: it's the same day and free! And shouldn't Christine get homeschool gymnastics on Wednesday afternoons, since her brothers' soccer dominates our evenings? Oh, and that worldview class at church seems too good to be true! But let's not forget the "normal" evening activities of church choirs, music lessons, and Awanas (Scripture memory)—not to mention that I went to Bible Study Fellowship one morning every week for eight years. Wow. Some years, my kids did so much school in the car that I called them "Road Scholars." Missing ingredient: school.

6. *Hungering for encouragement:* It can be a lonely world for homeschool moms. There is no one to say, "Your kids are awesome; here's an A" or "I think your child should be invited to this honors class." I must admit that I often heard of awards given or school rankings of similarly aged public school neighbors, and I would think, *I wish my kid got noticed*. I am embarrassed to say that I even sent the standardized test scores to the grandparents the first year of homeschool—just wishing someone would say, "You are doing a good job. Maybe you are not messing them up after all." I know Colossians 3:23 says to do all things for the glory of God, not man, so why does this desire creep back into me so often? *Can't I get just a little glory for me? Just a little glory for my kids?* Ha! Do I really forget *Who* is in charge of my homeschool? I have had to go back to that original list of *why to homeschool* so many times. One of the reasons I homeschool was not "So I can be recognized for doing a good job." It was not "So my child can get accolades from his peers." But the biggest reason was so my

> When we passed the place called Coffee and Crepes, my newly reading five-year-old said, "Who would name a place Coffee and Creeps?!"

child will hear, "Well done, my good and faithful servant." Missing ingredient: eternal focus.

7. *Being puffed up:* Too often on this journey, pride has reared its ugly head. It is difficult when taking a stand and walking against the crowd in any direction not to feel a bit of excitement when your way works! But the only reason that happens is because God is at work. There were times I think I was homeschooling to prove a point instead of to do what was right. When the negative "I'll show them" attitude wins over the "I'll serve the Lord" attitude, the fall awaits. 1 Samuel 2:3 (NIV) says, "Do not keep talking so proudly or let your mouth speak such arrogance, for the Lord is a God who knows, and by him deeds are weighed." This showed most clearly when we debated sending our oldest son to high school. We had various reasons that looked like this particular Christian school could be a good opportunity for Casey: more godly men leading as examples, competitive sports, Christian friends, etc. Casey asked us not to send him. My heart ached to have him (and frankly his good example) at home all day. Through prayer, we realized that we really felt it was the right thing to do for him and his well-being. Dark voices began echoing in my head, *But your identity is a homeschool mom of four! Everyone is going to know you "failed"! You're quitting! You must not have really believed what you set out to prove!* and on and on. Chris actively wanted Casey to go to high school but left the decision to me after his input. I analyzed five different ways of homeschooling through high school. I resisted the change in all of my normal ways—coming up with my plans B, C, and D. But one morning, in silent prayer (amazing how many realizations happen on that porch while the birds sing in my ear), I realized that it was meant to be. As my friend Ann Winters says, "God is always on Plan A—always." I called the school and arranged a tour. The following fall, I sat in the bleachers watching him play high school soccer as the only starting freshman, and a man came over to me and said, "Casey is the answer to my prayers for a friend for my son." I could hardly choke words out in reply. My prayers had been answered as well. Missing ingredient: humility to accept when God's plan wasn't my plan A.

> Prepare your children for heaven more than Harvard. Heaven lasts longer.

So when we add *laughter* to *great expectations*, *humility* with *contentment*, and some *home* along with *school*, I suppose we end up with homeschool. It sometimes looks like peanut butter mush, but sandwiched between two cookies of love, it is really delicious. Really!

God bless,

Terri

Huffin' and Puffin'

Dear Lindsey,

Trying to get out the door for travel soccer for my older two has always been a challenge—especially when my younger two were toddlers.

Once, on the way out the door, I heard a cry, "Mom, I need your help!" from the upstairs bathroom. As I ascended the staircase, the smell was overpowering. Knowing the smell was synonymous with "urgent mess" for me to clean up, I felt my heartbeat accelerate. *We are going to be late!* I thought, frustration rising. I knew this was hardly the toddler's fault, so I began praying that God would give me a calm spirit with the one at hand, that I would not take out my intense feelings on the child, since it was the timing—not his behavior—that was the issue.

As I arrived at the bathroom, I truly could not believe my eyes. There was the mess…all over him, his hands, the cupboard, the knobs, the sink, the spigot, the towels, and the light switch?! I was aghast! Seriously, the stench took away my ability to breathe. He was distraught in the middle of it all. It was clear my four-year-old had tried to clean himself after diarrhea.

It was then that I asked one of those "mom" questions that sounds so idiotic in retrospect because I knew the answer, but I just had to say something. "What happened?!" I tried to sound calmer than my heart rate would indicate.

Then God answered my prayers for calm as my rage turned to internal laughter. The toddler answered in despair: "I don't know. My belly was huffin' and puffin', and then it all just shot out like a rocket!"

Anger can't change the past, but laughter sure helps today.

I hope it helps your day!

Blessings,

Terri

> I just heard my six-year-old tell the dental hygienist: "I brush my teeth every night, except once two years ago when we got home too late and Mom wouldn't let me."

> My five-year-old: "I can whistle better in the afternoon because I'm awaker."

Turkey Tastes Better without Lily Pads

Dear Lindsey,

The westerly wind blew little waves into our lake, like marks of a knife on a frosted cake. It wasn't enough to cancel our beach day with my friend Sheri and her teenage girls, but it was enough that our normal boating and fishing were deterred.

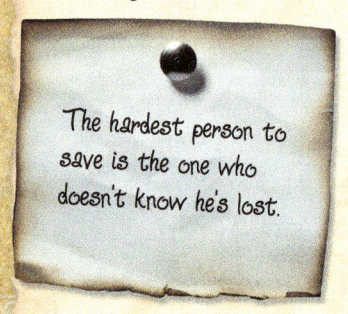

> The hardest person to save is the one who doesn't know he's lost.

We owned the entire perimeter of the forty-acre body of water that provided a home for bass, pike, bluegill, and countless turtles and frogs. The homemade sandy beach was perfect for fun family picnics, business events, and girlfriend days like this one.

"Can I go kayaking?" my five-year-old son asked. Kayaking was a newly acquired skill, and he was always one to love the kudos people gave him for being so athletic so young.

"It's windy. I don't think it would be much fun to have to fight it," I tried to deter the request. "Do you want to show them the trails?"

"I understand you don't want me to, but it's not that windy; I can handle it!" he pleaded.*

There was really no more danger in kayaking that day than other days. Though he was a good swimmer, his life jacket would provide extra safety from the water. The wind would be more of an inconvenience than a danger. So I pushed his boat into the water, and off he went!

His brother, three years older, followed. Within minutes, it was obvious to the elder that the wind was going to win the battle for the steering, so he returned and beached his kayak.

I looked out to see my youngster in a full-out struggle against the wind. His small stature kept him low in the boat—his armpits barely cresting the edge of the cavity where he sat. The special kayak oar (which has paddles on both ends, rotated ninety degrees from each other) was in full motion *OVER* his head. The cumbersome motion looked exhausting, as he paddled water on the left of the boat, then lifted the six-foot oar over his shoulders, twisted, and quickly put in to pull equal water on the other side. Under calmer waters, each stroke would have propelled the rider through the water almost endlessly like a friction-free glide. Not today.

Each stroke looked as though it took his entire body, down to his toes. He struggled against the wind. He rowed and rowed, trying to get to the west end of the lake. But the wind was too much, and it continued to pull him backwards.

After a few minutes, I asked my oldest son to get into the paddle boat (which kited less) and go save his naïve brother. Prepared with the rope and friends (Sheri's girls), he went to the rescue.

Sheri and I enjoyed our moment alone. Girl time is a gift that rarely comes with silence! I suppose I should not have been surprised when our peace turned into noise as a Brady brawl broke out on the water. I heard splashing and paddle smacking and screams of torment as the five-year-old rejected his brother's offer.

"Get out of here! I can do this by myself!"

Embarrassed by his behavior out of my reach, I calmly went to the side of the lake and told the rescuers to retreat. "I guess he doesn't want help," I explained.

They returned, and we continued our day of fun with friends—fire started, hot dogs ready, and Polaris Ranger full of gas for the trail tours.

I watched the lake, and my little guy was going east as fast as the wind was blowing. His tiny arms were no match for the forces from above. Soon, he "landed." The bed of lily pads at the east end of the lake held on to many of our lost fishing lures. Any boat without a motor surely ended there due to westerly winds, but in the kayak, it presented more trouble, since the oar could not get water amidst the weeds, even on a calm day. I knew he was stuck and going nowhere. I waited.

Then we heard it: a sound like a ghost moaning.

"Mrs. Brady, I think he's crying on the lake," the girls came to me, concerned.

"He's okay, or he would be asking for help," I said, trying to stay tough.

> "Being confident is telling yourself you're going to win. Being cocky is telling everybody else."
> —Casey Brady (age fifteen)

"Wooooaaaaaahhhh!" the moaning continued, getting louder.

"Are you sure he won't drown?" the nine-year-old girl asked.

"As long as I can hear his voice, I know he's above water," I joked, but then explained: "If you listen, his cry is getting louder. He's trying to get our attention, but I really just want to hear the words, 'I'm sorry. Please help me.' I believe if he sits long enough, he will realize the plight of his situation, and he will kindly ask for help." (And I quietly prayed that would be true!)

"Wah Wah Wah!" the noise reached full crying, and vocal cords were at a maximum.

"Mrs. Brady, don't you think we should go out there and *make* him come in?" the girls asked, so kindly caring about his well-being.

I debated for a minute. *I AM the mom,* I thought. *I could go win this battle with force and punish him for the rest of eternity!* But my senses kept coming back to me, *If he struggles long enough, he will recognize that he is NOT the one in control.*

Finally, the crying turned into intelligible words, "Mom!"

"Yes, dear?" I answered from the shore.

"Can you please help me?" he said, between sniffles.

"Of course! I will send your brother; but before he can tie your boat, you owe him an apology for trying to hit him with the oar, right?"

Silence, no answer…

"Say, 'Okay, Mom,'" I directed.

"Okay, Mom," he mumbled, almost resolved to his lack of control of this situation.

I listened for the proper words and attitude toward his rescuers upon their arrival to the kayak. Thanks and sorrys filled the air, replacing the space the moaning had occupied moments before.

As an adult, I wonder how many times I've had to end up "stuck in the lily pads" to learn my lesson.

Someone will cry out today, "Why is God letting me drown?!"
    Yet He's hearing every word and knows we're still breathing.

I've cried, "I can't handle this!"

And He already knew that. We are not meant to handle it.

I am sure my son must have been thinking, "Why won't Mom help me?!"
…when he had already batted away the very person I had sent to help because he wanted help from *anyone* but *that person*.

"Doesn't God hear my moaning and crying?!"
Yet He tells us He would rather hear "sorry," "thanks," and "please help me."

Pride.

- It's at the root of all conflict, according to John Maxwell.

- It *always* leads to fall, according to the Bible (Prov 16:18). Haughtiness is an abomination to the Lord! Yet, I battle it like an addiction.

- It is when we turn down the help—because "we don't need it."

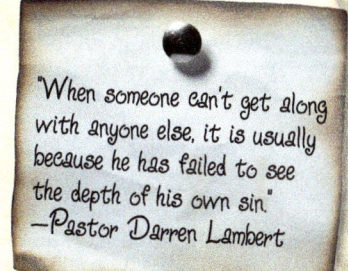

- It's when we say, "God isn't answering" because He's not solving the situation the way *we* think it should be solved.

- It's caring more about looking good to others than being good in God's sight.

> "When someone can't get along with anyone else, it is usually because he has failed to see the depth of his own sin."
> —Pastor Darren Lambert

God's power is made perfect in weakness (2 Cor 12:9), yet I've often laughed, *But do I really have to LOOK so weak? Ha-ha!*

As I write this, the holidays are approaching, which is when I seem to struggle with pride the most.

- Your husband is going to ask you to make his mom's recipe.
  - Hook your rope to her boat.

- Your sister-in-law is going to wipe the table exactly where you *just wiped*!
  - Tell her thank you.

- Your grandkids are going to spend more time with the other set of grandparents than you.
  - Thank God that He gave you grandchildren you love.

I really believe my best weight-loss program was when I realized the weight of the world was not on my shoulders, and it never was.

Come on, girl, you can do it! **Rise above being offended this year!**
Take the help and give the help. God has great plans.

Holiday turkey tastes better without lily pads.

Love ya,

Terri

"The Lord detests all the proud of heart. Be sure of this: They will not go unpunished." (Proverbs 16:5)

"Humble yourself before the Lord, and He will lift you up." (James 4:10)

"The men were amazed and asked, 'What kind of man is this? Even the winds and the waves obey him!'" (Matthew 8:27)

* Nice "wise appeal" from *Say Goodbye to Whining, Complaining, and Bad Attitudes…in You and Your Kids!* by Turansky and Miller.[25] Obviously, we had not reached the goals of that book by this point, but I am so grateful for the "wise appeal" in the Brady family!

Wanna Talk about Me!

Regarding gossip: "Loose lips sink ships" (friendships, relationships, and leaderships).

Dear Lindsey,

Will I ever keep my mouth shut?! I have thought after regretting an argument at an event with friends. The truth is the problem was not my mouth but my heart that was speaking. John Maxwell says pride is the reason for *all* conflict. The Bible says it comes before the fall. Pride develops through the way we view ourselves and will affect the number of relationship conflicts we have in life. In these next few letters, I hope to sharpen each other as iron sharpens iron, while we enjoy laughing (or gasping!) at stories of my prideful past, learn to diagnose an ego problem, and get to the *heart* of the matter.

Kids say the darnedest things! They tell the unmasked truth at times, like when my then six-year-old said, "Sometimes I feel like my friends aren't listening to me. It's like they are quiet when I talk, but they are only thinking of what they are going to say next."

Toby Keith's song makes me smile every time I hear it: "Wanna talk about me, wanna talk about I, wanna talk about number one, oh my me my!" In the song, he's talking about a girl he is dating who talks so much about herself that he never gets a chance to say anything.

I really don't even remember dating Toby Keith, but the song describes me (at least the "old me") so well! I even had a "grandma down in Alabama" (as the song states)![26]

Pride is defined as "a feeling of deep pleasure or satisfaction derived from one's own achievements" (or children's achievements or possessions), according to the dictionary. However, here's a possible Christian definition: "being full of self, and therefore having no room in the vessel to be full of God." Proverbs 11:2 says that "with humility comes wisdom" (NIV). Too often, we walk around so unwise.

Like a skirt accidentally tucked into nylons, revealing a woman's undergarments for an entire wedding reception dance, pride is a sin that is evident to all those around but is seemingly hidden from the bearer. I have heard that *EGO* stands for "Edging God Out." But when I first was figuring out my own pride problem, I loved God, and really, I figured I loved God more than most did, so I was safe from any ego issues. Ha! There was that pride again.

Pride destroys teams.

Whether it's a business team, a church team, a marriage, or a family, pride is a cancer that will starve the body. However, a problem cannot be solved until it is properly defined, and a prideful person, it seems, cannot see his own sin. *That's about others because I don't feel good about myself*, I can remember thinking *every* time I heard the word *pride*. This is where the reader is cautioned: we may be talking about *you*, and you don't know it! (Just kidding! We all know we are talking about the ones who would never read this letter!) All I know is that I am talking about me. *Pride is an addiction from which I am always recovering.*

I often hear people say that they have low self-esteem and not high self-esteem, and so therefore this problem is not applicable to them. Ironically, when I collected the symptoms of pride, and subsequently compared them to the symptoms of low self-esteem from Dennis Rainey's book *Building Your Mate's Self-Esteem*,[27] I couldn't believe how many of the symptoms were identical.

> Sometimes I feel like Gladys. Sometimes, I'm just the Pips. May God use me either way.

"How is that possible?" you may ask. "Aren't low self-esteem and high self-esteem opposites?"

In the middle of each description is the problem:

Self.

Whether low- or high-self-esteemed, if we esteem ourselves as anything other than God-esteemed, we are doomed to live lives of conflict.

That leads me to the first symptom of pride: talking about yourself.

I can change *any* subject back to me, and I used to think it was quite a talent! Imagine my conversations:

> Her: "We moved here from Colorado."
>
> Me: "I have family in Colorado."
>
> Her: "My child is really struggling in math."
>
> Me: "Oh that's funny; my son is acing math!"
>
> Her: "I had such a rough day today."
>
> Me: "Oh, I know; I hate Mondays."

I *hate* to think of myself having these conversations. How much could the Lord have done through me if instead I had been interested in the others' words? How the math student's mom could have been encouraged by words about *her*, not *me!* Maybe the "rough day" was looking for truly caring words: "I'm sorry to hear that! How can I help?" What if the one from Colorado was only wishing for someone to know that she was new to the area?

> *Whether low- or high-self-esteemed, if we esteem ourselves as anything other than God-esteemed, we are doomed to live lives of conflict.*

Pride: It leads to relationship conflict and edges God out.

So what now? What if, as we read the symptoms through the next letters, we identify an issue with pride—what next? Don't despair! God is bigger than the pride boogie man. Identifying the problem is half of the solution.

Ironically, I feel *very* confident writing about pride but not qualified to write about humility—which is the only solution. Reading C. J. Mahaney's book *Humility: True Greatness* provides the reader great perspective.[28]

However, for this first symptom (talking too much about oneself) the practical answer is obvious:

Talk less about yourself. Some will read this and think I am saying that we should *never* talk about ourselves; however, it is truly a matter of the heart. Are we listening to others? Are we caring about others? Or are we pushing opinions, experiences, and ourselves on others, trying to uplift ourselves?

Pray. Well…maybe that should have been #1. Since pride seems to be the king of invisible sins (invisible only to the beholder but visible to all others), we must ask God to open our eyes to where we are blind.

Think of others more than you think of yourself. C. S. Lewis said, "True humility is not thinking less of yourself, but thinking of yourself less."[29]

> "True humility is not thinking less of yourself, but thinking of yourself less." –C.S. Lewis

My husband says that a man doesn't marry a woman for her body, her brains, or any other part of her "self." He says he marries her because of how she makes him feel. It is the same in business relationships, friendships, and marriages alike: in relationships, our goal should *not* then be to make others think highly of us, but our goal should be to make them think highly of themselves, or better yet, think highly of our God when they are around us.

The most important commandment is to love the Lord your God with all your heart, soul, mind, and strength; and the second one is like it: to love your neighbor as yourself (see Matthew 22:37-40 and Mark 12:30-31). To truly love God, we will love His people. We will care about them and listen to them.

May we use our ears twice as much as our mouths today!

"Let every man be swift to hear, slow to speak" (James 1:19 KJV).

God bless,

Terri

Letters to Lindsey

Small Enough to Be Used (Whose Baby Is This?!)

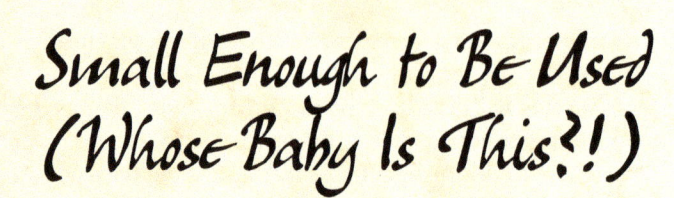

Dear Lindsey,

The Bible says, "...whoever humbles himself will be exalted," (Matthew 23:12). I say, "Humble yourself, or God will do it for you!" Hee! Whether it was falling in the church parking lot last month, finding underwear on fire on my chandelier while I had visitors, or forgetting someone was coming to my house for lunch that I cooked, these humbling experiences have all been reminders: I am not great.

> When I found my hair clip on my jewelry tree, I got the idea to look for my missing ring in my hair clips drawer. Found it.

Hudson Taylor, a nineteenth-century missionary to China and one of the most profound Christian thinkers of all time, had this to say about his life: "I often think that God must have been looking for someone small enough and weak enough for Him to use, and that He found me."

It's sad to me how often I have wanted to look better than I really am. That is the next symptom of an ego problem in this series of letters about pride:

Trying to Look Better than Reality or Being Stingy with "Sorry"

> Watching ESPN Sports Center, J.R. (age six) said, "You know what I don't like about TV? They are talking about Tim Tebow behind his back."

Let me illustrate: A "Polly Pocket" is like a Barbie who has been zapped by the *Honey, I Shrunk the Kids* gun, and her shoes were more impossible than Barbie's to find in the grass. The Cheerios and raisins that were supposed to have lasted through all four soccer games had also been dumped into said grass within this first game. The double stroller was loaded with activities and snacks for my younger two (ages two and one at the time) so that my older two could participate in a soccer tournament.

"I'll take the baby and meet you at field 10," Chris said as he pushed the stroller along the sideline toward our second son's game. I waited for the nine-year-old to finish in the coach's meeting while I pretended to do a Seek and Find game from the *Highlights* magazines of my youth, but it seemed impossible in this grass to find matching shoes for poor Polly.

I put the two-year-old on one hip, and the nine-year-old and I walked toward field 10 about four field-lengths away.

Thousands of people filled every soccer field's sideline of this event. The acreage allowed for more than thirty simultaneous games, so I was grateful to only need to go a distance of four fields. I could see Chris, already a couple of field-lengths ahead, struggling to move the stroller's wheels through the wet grass. There was a game on my right and left the entire walk, and as spectators yelled for their kids from every direction, I tried to squeeze between them.

> "We appreciate the magnitude of forgiveness more when we recognize the magnitude of our sin."
> —Casey Brady (age fifteen)

Suddenly, the game on my right halted, and the whistle blew. Three mothers went running onto the field. My heart sank; *there must be a major injury*. My mind raced, as I realized I had never even seen *one* mother run onto the field, much less *three*! I watched with anticipation, wondering if someone was badly hurt, or if there would be a catfight. (You never know with us soccer moms!)

One of the mothers in the center of the field turned in the direction of the crowd and said angrily, *"Whose baby is this?!"* as she held up a cute little one-year-old boy. To my horror, I realized it was *my* one-year-old boy the stranger was now holding!

I took a quick glance to see Chris still pushing a stroller a field away, not realizing his passenger had escaped.

I gathered my courage and picked my way through the sideline crowd to retrieve J.R. I told the mean lady, "I know his mother."

> Why was "Find my iPhone" invented before "Find my toddler"?!

Ha-ha! Just kidding. I didn't say that—but I thought about it.

How embarrassing!

Not only did we lose a child, but we didn't even know he was missing! Ugh!

I wish I had a video of *how* he got out of that stroller because it is still a mystery to us! Thousands of people there, and no one saw his escape? Wasn't the stroller still moving? Did he fall and then get back up and head for the field? Was he looking for me or just chasing another soccer ball?

The questions all remain unanswered.

That feeling though…the one where I wanted to explain to everyone how faultless I was in the story…the one where my embarrassment actually slowed my legs from making the steps toward retrieving my own son…the feeling that I cared more about what those strangers thought of me than what God thought…the feeling that prevented me from saying, "Sorry!" which clearly should have been the first word out of my mouth, regardless of the fault assigned to their inconvenience…the feeling that I wanted to look better than actuality showed me to be…

That's pride.

In my fun little "Brady classic," it is amusing to think of the embarrassment in the situation. In reality, though, pride becomes a problem when we start worrying more about what man thinks than what God thinks. We start living a facade that we are great and never want anyone to think otherwise. We buy clothes we can't afford, live in houses beyond our means, and avoid the words, "I'm sorry" because we're afraid of how they "make us look." We analyze fault to see if we believe ours weighs more than that of others involved before we determine whether we really have to apologize.

> Pride is the eclipse that blocks us from seeing the Son.

For me, though, in real relationships with real people, there is nothing that makes a person look better than when he or she apologizes and truly means it. Sincere apologies represent quiet strength. When one admits wrong, it clears the air and allows others the confidence to admit their wrongs as well. Stubbornness breeds stubbornness. As the song goes, "We all talk a different language talking in defense."[30] Admitting wrong breeds comfort for those around you, removes their defenses, and allows for more pure relationships.

May we be comfortable in being "small enough and weak enough" for God to use.

In love,

Terri

> Pride is the eclipse that blocks the Son from being seen by others around us.

Humble yourself before the Lord. (Don't make Him get out His "*Honey, I Shrunk the Kids*" gun and bring us down to size!)

"For it is written: 'I will destroy the wisdom of the wise; the intelligence of the intelligent I will frustrate.'" (1 Corinthians 1:19 NIV)

The Most Difficult Instrumentalist to Find

Dear Lindsey,

Her tears flowed next to me, while she tried to drain every ounce of joy from my victory. I know it was her high school senior year, but I had won even though I was a junior. Did she think I didn't deserve it? Didn't she know how many hours of preparation I had paid to get to this point?

It wasn't just that "I played the saxophone," I had *bought* the saxophone—or half of it anyway (my parents paid for the other half)—with money from *hours* (or *years!*) of babysitting. I had even gone to the tryout extremely sick. My fever registered 102 before school the previous day. But if we missed school on Friday, the school rules didn't allow participation in weekend activities; so I had ignored the fever (and avoided Mom's touch) and headed to school anyway.

I had bonded with my tryout music for six months, waiting for *this* Saturday, the tryout for District Band. I didn't even look for the thermometer that morning; I knew the fever was still there, but first chair would be selected to go to Regional Band, and then the first chair from each of the five regions would head to Pennsylvania State Band. My 2,000-student high school had not had a representative at the State Band level for the five previous years. What a hero I would be when I returned home with the coveted award, representing Carlisle High School! And that girl in the seat next to me was trying to steal my joy with her jealous tears. Our friendship was destroyed as I realized she didn't want good things to happen to me.

The next year, as God would have it, the tables turned. While I was laughing at someone who had tripped on the way into our jazz concert, my precious horn fell and was dented. The following day, I walked uphill both ways in a snowstorm (well, I did walk uphill, after my car wouldn't make it due to ice) to the repairman's shop in the basement of his neighborhood home. He fixed the horn the best he could, but the low B-flat wouldn't seal properly. I had two days to adjust to this handicap before County Band seat tryouts. Of course, I had nothing to worry about at County Band: I had made it to three levels higher than that the previous year. What were the chances of the judges choosing music for a tryout that would use the saxophone's lowest note anyway?

They did.

The seal didn't seal, and I, the previous year's State Band member, squeaked during the tryout. I was given second chair—which meant the solos of the concert would go to the other guy. He had not even advanced one level past County Band the year before. I was miserable to be "under" him.

Tears did not flow; I would *not* be that other girl! But I sat secretly brooding next to the young man who had been given first chair.

When it came time for the solo, jealousy had a grip on the reins of my heart. I hoped he would mess up. Crash! Fail!

He did fail. He didn't count right. (*See?!* I thought. *I deserved that place*.) The director told him where to play, and he came in wrong again. I leaned over and pointed to the music, showing him where the director meant for him to be. The first-chair player jerked and turned to me. Very upset, he said, "Just play the solo. You know he's going to give it to you as soon as I mess up!"

> After First-Class, Diamond Priority, Gold Priority, and the rest boarded the plane, we were called. Christine said, "Our group must be No Priority."

I suddenly realized I had stolen his joy, the same way I felt the girl had stolen mine the year before.

Jealousy is another symptom of an ego out of control, and it destroys relationships.

When the conductor of one city's philharmonic was asked to name the most difficult instrumentalist to find for his orchestra, he didn't answer "oboe" or "French horn" as I would have expected. He didn't even hesitate to think when he replied, "Second fiddle."

Sinful human nature wants to get first chair and take credit for getting there. Wasn't it God who gave me the ability to play an instrument? Didn't He give me the desire to practice hard and the time to do it (Philippians 2:13)? Didn't He allow me the babysitting jobs to earn the money to buy the instrument and then fix it? Did orphans in a third-world country have any of these choices? Without Him, would I have had ears to hear music or fingers to form the tones? From another angle, isn't He sovereign? Didn't He allow the saxophone to break, the judges to pick that part of the song, the squeak to emit from my horn, and the other young man to be chosen?

> "Lift up the rock of irrational, overblown...criticism and you will see the roach of jealousy scurrying away from the light."
> —Mark Driscoll

Jealousy destroys relationships. It is ultimately a form of lack of faith in God, and like any symptom of pride, it blocks us from fellowship with the Lord. We are not loving God with "all our mind" if we are using our mind to think of why we deserve something more than He gave us. I have heard of mothers jealous of daughters, wives jealous of husbands, siblings jealous of each other—and all of those can be within one house, being torn apart by its inhabitants.

- Jealousy says, "I know more than God" (because I believe I would have been better suited for these gifts).

- Jealousy says, "I care more about myself than I do about the person who was blessed with what I want."

- Jealousy is the antithesis of loving God and our neighbor as we are commanded.

> "You will never be something God can use until you are nothing but worthless dirt begging for mercy."
> —Dr. Gary Hallquist

So how do we overcome jealousy?

1. Pray!

Satan, get thee behind me! We will not be tempted beyond what we can bear (1 Corinthians 10:13).

2. Replace bad thoughts with good ones.

It is virtually impossible to say, "I will not think that anymore," because human sinful nature allows the thoughts to creep back. Instead, *replace* the thoughts with positive ones. Congratulate the person who got the position or reward; obviously, you admired the position enough to want it for yourself.

3. Thank God (1 Thessalonians 5:18).

A thankful heart cannot be a jealous one. Thank God for what you *do* have instead of focusing on what you don't. Thank God for second fiddles! Without them, there would be no musical harmony. When we are thanking God for what He has done, we are *not* telling God what to do.

We are so blessed to have been given *any* part to play in His orchestra. For His glory, may we play our part well.

In love,

Terri

> J.R. (age six) to his brother in the car: "My heart always hurts so much until I say I'm sorry when I need to."

"As it is, there are many parts, but one body. The eye cannot say to the hand, 'I don't need you!' And the head cannot say to the feet, 'I don't need you!' On the contrary, those parts of the body that seem to be weaker are indispensable, and the parts that we think are less honorable we treat with special honor. And the parts that are unpresentable are treated with special modesty, while our presentable parts need no special treatment. But God has combined the members of the body and has given greater honor to the parts that lacked it, so that there should be no division in the body, but that its parts should have equal concern for each other. If one part suffers, every part suffers with it; if one part is honored, every part rejoices with it. Now you are the body of Christ, and each one of you is a part of it." (1 Corinthians 12:20–27 NIV)

Stop in the Name of the Law

Dear Lindsey,

"*G*asp!"

Okay, now that you got that out of the way, I can share the story that made you do it.

As we continue this series on symptoms of pride/ego, I can go back a few decades to high school again. Unfortunately, I can probably think of more recent examples, but my pride couldn't handle sharing those; it's easier to think it was only a problem of my youth.

Next symptom: thinking I am above the law.

My high school's shop teacher, a former US Army colonel, was my neighbor, and he had a cute little poodle, Cocoa. For easy cash, I often took care of Cocoa when his owners were out of town. Rather than walking down the block to my house when he returned from his trip, the colonel (as we students called him) chose to pay me when he saw me in the school cafeteria on the Monday after my pet sitting.

This led to many jokes of which the colonel was unaware:

He would approach my lunch table full of teens of both genders, hand me money, and say, "Thanks for last night," or "This is for the weekend."

As he left, snickers would fill our table. Soon, they would see him coming and get silent to see what words he would use when he handed me cash: "Here he comes to pay Terri for her 'services.' Be quiet!"

I never mentioned the torture to him, but I cringed each time he approached.

One weekend, the colonel had asked me to pet sit, but after accepting the job, I realized I had a commitment to go somewhere with my family for the weekend. I forgot to tell him that I was unable to keep poor little Cocoa. I didn't remember until Monday morning when he approached my lunch table.

The table hushed in anticipation of his words.

"Thanks for the weekend," he said as he slid a ten-dollar bill into my hand in front of my friends.

I gulped.

I must have forgotten to tell him I couldn't take care of his dog.

My heart raced, but my ego ignored the urge. "You're welcome," I said and took the cash, hoping the colonel would disappear quickly.

He never asked me to take care of Cocoa again.

During my senior year, my parents (not knowing this story) suggested I have the colonel write a recommendation for me for college, since a US Army colonel would be a good advocate to have. "No, thanks," I said.

How I wish I could go back and change what I did! The colonel knew I hadn't taken care of that dog. I can only imagine the damage in his house when he returned. A starving, thirsty dog probably left messes all over and destroyed anything in its path. I don't know why the colonel chose to see if I would be a big enough person to admit it; maybe he knew the years of guilt would be worse than the verbal confrontation. I have tried searching for him online several times in my adulthood so I could apologize—to no avail. God has forgiven me, but forgiving myself has taken longer.

"Better that your heart should have no words than your words have no heart."
—Chris Brady

I don't know why I thought God's commandment against lying (Exodus 20) didn't apply to me, but I did.

I can remember justifying the fib in my mind the following week:

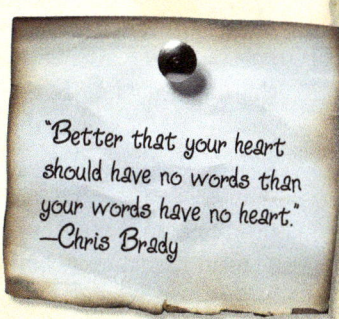

- What was I supposed to do? Everyone was listening!
- I didn't really *lie* per se; I just said, "You're welcome." (Note: It's still bearing false witness.)
- It was only ten dollars.
- It's just a dog.

Ugh.

Thinking a law (especially a law of God) doesn't apply to me is a symptom of pride.

When telling a negative story, I prefer to use myself as the example, so I can use others as positive examples. But obviously in this world, there are many examples of actors, business owners, and presidents who have had an ego that caused them to put themselves above a law…or two.

Huge scandals begin with a small thought in a heart. One little lie because it was only ten dollars leads to millions unless the ego gets under control.

- "I deserve to take these supplies home from work, and no one notices anyway" is only an attempt to justify stealing.
- "I can watch these movies because I am an adult now" justifies adultery.
- "I am running late because of traffic" (when really we left our house later than we should have and happened to also run into traffic) *or* "I'll be there in ten minutes" (when we know it will really be twenty, but we don't want the appointment to leave) is still lying.
- "That rule doesn't apply to me because I am so important to this team" is taking advantage of our blessings.

Thanks to an analogy from my husband, Chris, I have often imagined that one day God will play the movie of my life back to review my behavior while I watch beside Him. My stomach churning would never allow for popcorn during that movie. I imagine that it is *my* life and no one else can be seen in the film. My heart has a voice in the movie, so my words, thoughts, and actions are of equal volume, but the circumstances around the words, thoughts, and actions cannot be seen, only the deeds for which I am responsible. My legs weaken when I see the laws that I took so lightly, thinking I was only doing what "anyone would do." I do not like myself in so many of the scenes of those home movies.

Thankfully, God is not done with me yet.

We can repent of our sins and ask forgiveness from those whom we have hurt (Acts 3:19). He can make us white as snow again (Isaiah 1:18). Repentance begins with recognizing the need for repentance. *Pride blocks recognition of our own sin and our need of a Savior.* Pride is the eclipse that blocks the Son from being seen. May I decrease that He may increase (John 3:30), and with that decrease, I can recognize that I am above no law.

Although God's laws have no exceptions (Hebrews 10:16), neither does His grace (Lamentations 3:22; Hebrews 4:16; Ephesians 2:4). Believe in forgiveness through the Lord Jesus Christ, and you will be saved (Acts 16:31). Wow! God is amazing!

I guess it's becoming obvious that the ramifications of one's ego/pride go far beyond the affairs of this life and into eternity. May we gain strength to live with eternal perspective, always.

God bless,

Terri

Climb the Ladder

Dear Lindsey,

*"When I survey the wondrous cross
On which the Prince of Glory died
My richest gain I count but loss
And pour contempt on all my pride."*[31]

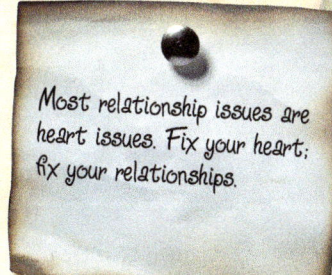

Most relationship issues are heart issues. Fix your heart; fix your relationships.

I wrote the words to that old hymn from Isaac Watts in my journal while I fought back internal emotional pain. I *wanted* to pour contempt on all my pride, but it kept haunting its possessor.

Then I decided to really try to "survey the wondrous cross," and during my quiet time that morning, I went into a little daydream that I will never forget. It was a daydream that forced the surrender of my heart, once again.

In the distance, I saw not one but three crosses on the hill. A crowd of people surrounded the base. There was noise…people's voices, but I couldn't understand what they were saying.

I stared at the center cross as I walked closer, praying that I would stay focused on Him, despite the distractions of this crazy surrounding world. I wanted to "be one" with other people as He was one with God so that people would know why He came, yet I battled conflict in my heart. I wanted to survey that wondrous cross and leave the conflict behind.

I saw guards, Roman I assumed, in costume as the movies had portrayed. Some spectators on the hill were on their knees, in a deep mourning wail. Others were shouting insults toward the cross. Others were simply walking away, not able (or perhaps not willing) to "survey" any longer.

I looked at His face. Jesus's eyes were still open. He looked down on all the people—those crying, those shouting, and even those leaving—and I remembered His words, "Forgive them; they know not what they do."

What wondrous love is this, that He could forgive even in agony?

> Agony caused by lashes of a whip tied especially for breaking skin on His bare back while officers held His flesh taut for maximum tearing.

> > Agony caused by friends, even His closest, who had deserted Him. One had betrayed with a kiss, others with their departure or denial.

> > > Agony caused by a crown of thorns forced onto His head to pierce the skin while they mocked Him as a "king."

> > > > Agony caused by taunting hours before, "If you are so great, why don't you tell us who hit you?" as they struck His blindfolded face.

I imagined how He must have felt as people sang, "Hosanna!" at His coming to town, so grateful for His arrival; then in contradiction, people screamed, "Crucify Him!" just days later, treating Him like the criminals on the adjacent crosses.

How did He keep from fighting back? I wondered when I recalled his accusers bringing Him to Pontius Pilate, telling the lies that He had denounced taxes and that He was undermining the government (see Luke 23). He stayed focused on His message: He was the Son of God. When King Herod tried Him, Jesus never even spoke, as if wrestling with the pig wasn't worth words. He was at peace with allowing God's will to be done through Him. *Why can't I do that?!* I wondered.

Crucifixion, a slow, lingering electric chair of the era, was public, naked, and profoundly cruel. There was no way to "look good" even as the Son of God hanging on that wood. Nails pierced His hands and feet.

Three men died that day at Calvary. One on the cross next to Jesus jeered at Him, while the other, in full belief said, "Jesus, remember me when You come into Your kingdom." That is when Jesus told him, "I tell you the truth: today you will be with Me in paradise."

I broke out of the dream and thought about myself again. I could see me saying, "I'm kind of having a bad day here. My emotions are out of control; I'd really like some time on this cross where I don't have to deal with you people." Yet Christ had a message to relay (that heaven awaits anyone who believes) even in his last hour.

My daydreaming continued, and I found a ladder. I set it next to Jesus's cross and began to climb. I wanted to *survey* the Savior.

The sweat, mixed with blood, poured from His body. I recalled His "sweating blood" during a deep prayer just the night before, though His closest friends' loyalty faded in sleep. I meditated on the fact that even *He* asked His heavenly Father for a change of the Plan, yet what He wanted was that God's will be done.

The daydream paused as personal thoughts came in: *That's what I want: God's will to be done! Yet there's so much conflict; how can it be?*

In my daydream, my actions continued. I wanted to get closer—to talk to Jesus as He hung on that cross, looking down on the people. "Did e'er such love and sorrow meet?" came to mind from another verse of the same hymn.

From His view, I could see His accusers—and mine, too. "He died for them, also," I was reminded.

I leaned toward Him to whisper, brought my lips close to His ear, and tried to form words. Thoughts flooded my mind. *I can't believe I can talk to You! This is amazing!* It was then that I remembered the concerns on my heart that day—the ones I had wanted to talk to Jesus about that morning, and I said into His bleeding ear:

> "Jesus, *she* won't return my phone call!"
>
> "Jesus, I am so jealous that I didn't get what I wanted."
>
> "Jesus, I have been wronged, and they are going to make me look bad."

I forced myself out of the daydream, realizing the lack of reality in thinking I would *ever* say that to Him as *He* hung there. How petty my prayers seemed that morning now that I had *truly* surveyed Him! How selfish! He died for me; can't I live a moment for Him? I slid back into the daydream, recognizing that the only thoughts that could come to mind to whisper in His ear as He hung on that cross were unsaid, choked by tears:

"I am *so* unworthy."

"I am so sorry."

"Thank you."

He glanced in my direction as if to answer my unspoken words, "I know. It's why I came."

I snapped out of my daydream, and tears flowed as I contemplated how petty my prayers had been that morning.

> *He gave His life for me; can't I live a moment for Him?*

- When my pride gets in the way, I climb the ladder.
- When I feel I have been wronged, I climb that ladder.
- When I am jealous, I climb the ladder.
- If I am talking too much about myself, I need to climb that ladder.
- If I am feeling perfect, qualified to start correcting others, I climb the ladder.
- If I am more worried about the scrutiny of man than the scrutiny of God, I *climb the ladder*.

Are my thoughts worthy of whispering in His ear from the top of the ladder?

Whisper in His ear about the parents who just lost children this week. He cares.

Pray to Him about the woman lost in the dark world of depression. He's holding her.

Ask Him in His ear how best to be His testimony in this lost world, and He would be relieved to know someone read His words so they would outlast His agony.

I had "open heart surgery" that morning. I surrendered. His will be done.

The whole world is in His hands, not mine, and that is where it needs to stay.

I pray that we may be *one* so the world will know that the Lord above sent Jesus Christ as our Savior (John 17:21): He humbled Himself to human birth—in a stable; He submitted to baptism—by another man; He washed filthy feet—for no one was lower than He; He died a criminal's death—alongside criminals, for God's glory. May we follow His example to true humility; I am above nothing. Peace on earth comes into our hearts when we can rest in God's will being done.

And if conflict arises, even if only inside us, may we climb the ladder to rise above the offense, survey the cross, and take time to whisper in His ear, "Thank You."

With love,

Terri

Summary of Pride/Ego Symptoms:

- Talking too much about oneself
- Wanting to correct others
- Caring too much about what people think/resisting apology
- Being secretly jealous/feeling "under blessed"
- Taking laws lightly
- Refusing to forgive/harboring bitterness
- Ranking people as more or less valuable than one another
- Talking down about others (closely related to talking about oneself)
- Resisting new information

"I'm Glad I'm a Boy!"

Dear Lindsey,

I love when kids say cute things!

While on vacation in Italy, somehow in the transition between hotels, we lost our bottle of hair conditioner. Christine (age eight) thought the hotel's provided body wash was conditioner, but instead of detangling and making her hair smooth, it made it into a sticky ball of rats' nests. She was sad that we would have to work through it, when Nate told me that he didn't know what the big deal was; he always used the body

I'm not sure if I like Twitter. I always feel like someone is following me.

wash on his hair, and it never bothered him. Casey quickly jumped in, "I use hair shampoo for everything; I don't know why we need different products."

I told them, "Well, boys can do that; girls need products!"

To which J.R. (age seven) said, "Yay! I'm glad I'm a boy! Except I guess I wouldn't get a lifeboat if my ship were sinking."

Smiles,

Terri

> When J.R. (age seven) overheard a soccer coach talking, J.R. said, "That guy reminds me of Dad—talking about history and courage."

Keep Planting

Dear Lindsey,

New Year's Day was unseasonably toasty as the record-warm winter reached its mid-season celebration. Just one year before, our North Carolina hometown had had its first white Christmas in fifty years. What a contrast that was to the seventy-degree sunshine that now crowned my head as I headed outside on January 1!

Being relatively new to North Carolina, I was elated by the weather. The contrast to the northern gray skies to which I had become accustomed, living north of the Mason-Dixon line most of my life, was enough to make me sing! I love the outdoors, and the blue sky lured me from my family room, still decorated with evidence of torn Christmas wrapping paper.

The warmth made it seem like I should be gardening, though the threat of frost could not be far around the corner; it was January after all, despite the day's forecast. I remembered I had bulbs to plant—the perfect solution to my garden craving, since they required weeks of cold before they could bloom.

As a clever housewarming gift, my parents had sent bulbs from their Colorado garden. I grabbed my bulb planter from the garage while dreams of tulips, lilies, and daffodils danced in my head.

Unlabeled upon arrival, these seeds would each present a surprise color as they emerged from the ground in six or eight weeks. The love of gardening was passed to me by my father, who was raised on a Kansas farm, where his mother, ninety-seven, still lives and gardens. Now I would have a piece of my parents' garden in my own, like a cycle of life that would continue to keep giving, year after year.

I was in a dreamy mood. That morning's church service was full of praise to God for giving us another year of life, and the gifts that it included.

I sang.

No, I didn't have an iPod plugged into my ears. I was alone with my tools, the unwrapped bulbs from my parents, and the dirt from God. I began the project.

"This is my Father's world...." I sang three verses while I planted His seeds in His soil and sprinkled them with water He provided. My knee cushion had the worth of gold, as I scooted it sideways on the backyard path, planting a pattern of what I assumed would become tulips. I sang and "painted" a rectangle, matching the bricks that encompassed.

I moved to the next flower bed, with what looked like eighty more bulbs in the shipping box. Scattering bulbs down either side of the stone walkway, I hoped for a beautiful array of color by spring. I imagined looking out the back windows from my homeschool room.

"In the rustling grass, I hear Him pass. He speaks to me everywhere,"[32] I sang.

Wow. I really had no idea how far a hundred bulbs would go, nor how much effort it took to dig a hole for each one! Two flower beds done, and I still had at least sixty bulbs!

I moved to the front of the house. This time, I dug large holes and tossed a smattering of bulbs into each. I figured this "confetti" look would be good out near the road, in front of the backdrop of the hedges, which seemed boring in contrast.

"Great is Thy faithfulness!"[33] I sang another hymn as I dug holes in pure clay. Thinking of Jesus's words from Matthew 13, regarding the seed growing in the proper soil, I filled the cavities with some potting soil to better provide for the smattering of bulbs in each.

Twenty bulbs left, and my shoulders ached. My knees didn't want to bend back into the position for digging. My working sweat was giving me a chill as the temperature dropped with the sun. I pushed on, not knowing the weather forecast for the following day. *"Day by day and with each passing moment, strength I find to meet my trials there…"*[34] came the song out of my mouth, as I forced my body into much-needed work to overcome the holiday sedentary state in which I had been. The songs rang through my ears, and I praised God for the gift of a beautiful day, and the colorful hope that each seed represented.

One hundred bulbs done.

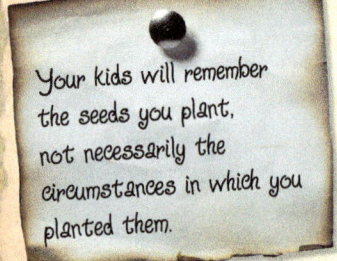

And I rested.

> Your kids will remember the seeds you plant, not necessarily the circumstances in which you planted them.

One week after that worship-filled Sunday for which I praised God, I looked outside to see a pattern.

There was a dark pattern around the rectangle perimeter of the backyard flowerbed. Dark spots lined each side of the stepping-stones.

Were the flowers starting to emerge already, in just one week?

I went out the front door to check on the others, and the dark spots were there, too. Large *holes* broke up the potting soil next to the hedges, and *holes* were in the woodchips lining the sidewalk to the door.

Something had eaten the bulbs!

I raced around to the back of the house, and to my dismay, the holes continued.

Like some horror flick, "holes" made a pattern as if leading me to the culprit, but no culprit was to be found.

I felt as if a thief had come in the night and destroyed my hope for a colorful spring. All the times in the past when I had enjoyed watching a squirrel run in the grass, a raccoon race up the tree, or a fox or deer relax in my backyard became negative thoughts as I blamed them all, not sure which one was so selfish as to steal my dream!

I wasted my New Year's Day! I thought, just as I heard a favorite song on Pandora: *"I'm smellin' coffee. Birds are singing just outside!"*[35] Chris Rice carried the tune, which I recognized as one that I had happily hummed the day I had planted the bulbs.

No, I guess I hadn't wasted New Year's Day. No person (or animal!) could take away the joy-filled day I had had: grateful for the gift my parents had given me, happy to be singing of "My Father's World." *I had enjoyed the planting.*

It reminds me of a John Maxwell saying: "Success shouldn't be measured by the harvest that we reap, but by the seeds that we plant."[36]

I am not naïve enough to believe that every seed that I plant in my children, my husband, my brothers- and sisters-in-Christ, and my neighbors will bring a harvest. But I want to be naïve enough to enjoy the planting anyway. We are responsible for the planting, but only God can make them grow.

First Corinthians 3:7 (NIV) says, "So neither the one who plants nor the one who waters is anything, but only God, who makes things grow."

And grow they did!

Six weeks later, as spring arrived, the same pattern became visible: the rectangular bed, the stoned path, the smattering in the hedges, all in a beautiful array of colors. I don't know if the animal had decided to leave pieces behind, or if the pieces he had taken were too insignificant to affect the overall painting, but God had made the right seeds grow in the right time.

He always does.

May He bless your days of planting for Him,

Terri

Raising Readers

The man who does not read good books has no advantage over the man who cannot read them.
—Mark Twain

Dear Lindsey,

I took three of my kids to the dentist this week—the normal every-six-months habit. We walked into the waiting room, books in hand. (Aside: I really believe if I bring my book, my wait is less. If I forget my book, the wait is longer. It is like a Murphy's Law for me!) The television had been playing to an empty room and was set to a morning talk show. A commercial came on with a famous female commentator asking a woman, "Did you kiss her? Did you like it?" I had no idea what was coming, but I quickly jumped up to turn off the television. When I spun to look at my kids, they were all three looking down at their books. Whew! One more day without that media educating my children's morals…I think.

I was enjoying the silence when an employee sprang into the room, remote in hand. "Oh, sorry! Here, let me put it on a kids' channel." And with all good intentions, she made the noise begin again, this time with cartoons flying.

> "Mom, when I am president, I will fix the USA and China. I will have the USA make China's toys, and then we will have money to send to China."
> —my six-year-old

From the waiting room, we went to the dentist chairs, where we each had our own personal TV. Mine was set on one of those "insider" shows that tells all the gossip about famous people. I quietly prayed for my children's ears…and for the actor about whom they were talking on my TV, who was in trouble for protecting his own children from his paparazzi.

After my appointment, I went to the waiting room, where my children were. Their books were open, while the television continued in the background. The receptionist asked, "How do you get them to do that?" as if it were taught as a dog trick, like playing dead.

How Do You Get Kids to Read?

Casey, our oldest, was quite a natural reader. He was reading well by the time he was five.

My next son was not quite the "natural," unless it was playing soccer. He was taught to read using the same method: *Teach Your Child to Read in 100 Easy Lessons*.[37] Only, I had to repeat every lesson at least once before going to the next, so I changed the title to *200 Torturous Lessons* and skipped the writing part of it until he was seven!

Now both boys and their younger siblings really enjoy reading. I can't even pretend to know all the answers to the question, "How do you get kids to read?" but I thought I would write down some of the things that, by the grace of God, seemed to help mine develop into readers. I humbly hope that it helps others grow bookworms in their own homes as well.

Things we have done:

Model reading for them: Children learn best by example. What you do speaks much more loudly than what you tell them to do.

Chris and Christine, reading side-by-side on an airplane

Read aloud to them: We were blessed to hear that advice when our children were babies, so we have been reading aloud to them since before they could speak. Even though they are all independent readers now, we still try to read several books a year as a family. We finished *Best Christmas Pageant Ever* last week (Okay, that one was really for *me!* I laugh and cry!) and right now are in Dickens's *A Christmas Carol*, as part of our traditions. We try to read aloud the Bible stories daily, as listed in the back of *Thomas Jefferson Education*. When I read *The Hiding Place*, about Corrie Ten Boom's efforts of saving Jews during the Nazi occupation, and her own time in the concentration camp, something that really stuck with me was that her father spent time every night reading aloud to the family—and she was in her thirties![38]

Library trips: We aim for minimally every three weeks, and they may each get ten books, which they are "supposed" to keep in their library book bag. Yes, that is forty borrowed books. There have been *many* times that I have literally set the timer on my phone for fifteen minutes. We disperse and meet at checkout when the timer goes off. I figure fifteen minutes is better than nothing! We recently found our church's library has a fantastic selection of preapproved series for youth.

Used-book stores: Wow! This gold-digging began as Chris trying to help me out when I had babies, but it has become almost a rite of passage to be old enough (and a good enough reader) to go to the used-book store with Dad.

Popcorn and hot chocolate: Yep food always gets me. One summer, when it was 87 degrees here in North Carolina, my seven-year-old daughter said, "Can we light the fire and pop some popcorn?" She has happy memories of our reading times in front of the fire! She had forgotten that those were in the Michigan winter! At our former home, we actually had a popcorn oil "fog" on the carpet in front of the fireplace, from the number of times we had taken our book bags by the fire.

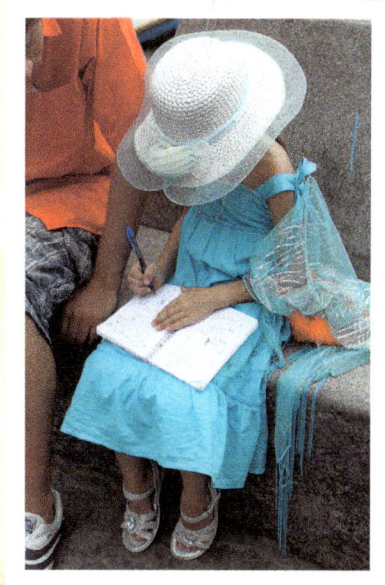

Christine in her "travel gear," journaling

Family reading night: You've heard of family game night and family movie night; why not family reading night?!

Book journals: This one goes in and out of our life. We just forget to write things down. Right now, Christine (age eight) has a poster that she has made, keeping track of the books she is reading.

Start a Parent/Child Book Discussion: Whether it is just you and your child(ren) or whether you invite other families to join you, reading a book and discussing it is fun and will draw you and your children together. I am always shocked…always…at the different ways my children see the book.

Reward with Books/Reading Time: Treat it like dessert, and they will see it as dessert. Treat is like it's a chore, and they will act like it. Give books as gifts, or rewards. A "trip to the library" is actually a coupon my kids can get for an A+ math test in our homeschool. Some nights, after we say bedtime prayers, they are allowed to read until a specified time. If they get to bed faster, they have more time to read. When they are around age six, I have often said, "Read in bed as late as you want." They are excited they get to stay up, so they push themselves in their reading ability and then fall asleep.

Fun!: The idea is to make a positive experience with reading. Get a flashlight and hang out in the blanket fort with the books. Put Post-it notes with book titles that have been read up on the wall, or put a quarter in a jar every time a book is read; then have ice cream or pizza with the proceeds when you reach a goal. (Food again!)

Limiting the "Diet": When trying to lose weight or even maintain health, it makes sense to count the calories and make the calories count. Wasted calories of cookies and chips turn to "waisted" calories, with zero nutritional gain. It is easier to turn to the fruits and veggies if they are the easiest-to-reach items in the kitchen. On the contrary, it is more difficult to get to the chips and cookies if they are not even in the house.

> My seven-year-old: "I like history because I want to become history." Smart girl!

It seems to me that we parents have a responsibility to limit the "electronic diet" of children. Video games, movies, and television are like chips and cookies. They take up the calories (hours spent) without yielding nutritional gain.

Look at these statistics:

> Number of minutes per week that parents spend in meaningful conversation with their children: 3.5

> Number of minutes per week that the average child watches screens: 1,680

> Percentage of day care centers that use screens for unsupervised child-entertainment during a typical day: 70

> Percentage of parents who would like to limit their children's screen time: 73

> Percentage of four- to six-year-olds who, when asked to choose between playing on a screen device and spending time with their fathers, preferred screens: 54

> Hours per year the average American youth spends in school: 900

> Hours per year the average American youth spends on screens: 1,500

If I had to choose a single thing in this letter that most likely had the biggest impact on our children's reading, it would be "limiting the electronic diet."

We are far from perfect. Limiting electronics has been difficult and continues to be. Reading requires a higher degree of mental participation than watching a movie, listening to music, or playing a video game, so it meets resistance. But you are the mom! You can do it!

With new babies, you can start fresh—read aloud; avoid buying electronics. But for those who have been more in the electronics world, it will take more discipline to make the shift. Rome was not built in a day.

- Maybe start with fifteen minutes one day each week of popcorn and reading time. Then make it longer or add another day. Set a goal at which to aim: One hour a day? Three hours a day? Three hours a week? You are the parent.

Aah! My dryer's lint screen was full of grass—a sign of SPRING and probably a sign of a lack of video games, too. Yay!

"I'd like to be the 'perfect' mom, but I'm too busy raising my kids." —unknown

- Have a daily limit on electronics with or without required reading. Again, have a goal, and start toward it with increments that make sense for your family.

- When beginning to increase reading time, we allow the children to choose from our selections or a whole section of the library, so they feel control in the options. Anything we as parents "force" assumes we expect "equal and opposite force." Our goal is for them to desire it, not necessarily just succumb to it. Making it their idea (or at least partially their idea by letting them choose books) gets them pulling instead of us just pushing. Later, we can add more content direction, such as "One hour of your book and then one hour of this book I want you to read."

Casey (age fourteen) and Nate (age eleven) reading books they bought for their Kindles. (This shot wasn't even staged!)

One note: I went through a time when I rewarded them with video game time for reading. Rewarding them with fifteen minutes of "educational computer play" time for every thirty minutes of reading did two things, according to Dr. James Dobson: First, it labeled reading the chore and computers the fun. Second, it was as though I was saying, "If I eat two salads, I get a dessert"—counterproductive in anyone's calorie counting. So we separated the electronic game time and decided to allow it one day per week.

Every so often, I come across something like a math program on the computer that would really help school. I try not to throw this baby out with the electronics' bath water. But if the electronics (even if educational) adversely affect the reading time, then we adjust.

Finally, I find myself being the "mom taxi" throughout the evenings, going from soccer practice to music lessons, etc. Sometimes, we have talked about everything there is to discuss while driving—or waiting to drive some more! As a child, I was never able to read in the car due to motion sickness, but my children use this time productively. Book lights have been a blessing, and if queasiness happens, they take a break with eyes closed. It's no excuse to turn on the DVD player hanging from the ceiling.

Tomorrow's leaders are today's readers. Let's raise them together, girlfriend!

Love ya,

Terri

"Mom, I Bet You CanNOT Do It"

Dear Lindsey,

Potty training toddlers was so fun! and not! all at the same time. I remember sticking strongly to a Bible verse, Romans 8:38–39: "For I am persuaded that neither death nor life, nor angels nor principalities, nor powers, nor two-year-olds, nor tantrums (mine), nor wet pants, nor lateness, nor hidden surprises, nor embarrassing moments on the play place, nor things present (when they shouldn't be), nor things to come, shall be able to separate me from the love of God" (or something like that).

Somewhere near the second birthday seemed to be the logical time to stop changing diapers. It was time for potty training! After all, my first child woke up one day (after we had read a couple of potty subject books) at the age of two and said, "I need to use the bathroom," and that was it! It was a piece of cake! Obviously, I had this motherhood thing accomplished, and I could teach anything!

Then came my second child, and his second birthday. He didn't quite read the book with me because he wouldn't sit long enough to hear anything. He would run around the room while I read aloud, hoping that if I kept reading, one day, he would be interested and look at a book. He did—when he was about five!

He never woke up and told me he needed to use the bathroom, so I started telling him.

>   It didn't work.

I got Skittles, lots of them.

>   It didn't work.

I set the timer and walked him to the bathroom every twenty minutes.

>   It didn't work.

> My exhausted daughter (age seven) said through tears, "I am so tired! My heart has been at the edge of a cliff, and it just went over. Wah hah hah!"

At one point, he stood under the piano in my living room and excitedly said, "Hey, Mom! It's a good thing I have on waterproof shoes because I just put number one all over them!"

He just wasn't getting it.

He wasn't "behind" for his age. His motor skills were amazing. At two and a half, he was in the pool, and he asked to take his water wings off. My husband and I thought it was a good time for some swimming lessons, so we stood close to each other. My husband put him in the position to swim and aimed him at me, three feet away, ready to scoop him up as he choked, like most kids do when beginning. Not him. He put his face down and swam toward me but avoided my arms and went *around* me to get to the side of the pool. He reached his arm up onto the edge and then turned to his five-year-old brother and said, "Let's race!"

But he preferred to go number one in his pants.

He taught himself the "flippy dive." (He named it, too.) He would stand on the edge of the pool, and do a front flip into the water, giggling the whole way. (Yes, I said age two!) Once, when we were staying at a hotel, a man thought I wasn't watching, and the heroic stranger almost jumped in after him, thinking he needed to be saved since he was so small. The man was surprised.

But the flippy-diver chose not to keep his pants dry.

At three, he began riding a two-wheel bike. We lived at the end of a cul-de-sac, which joined another cul-de-sac for a great figure-eight racing track. He would spend hours racing with the five- and eight-year-olds going around that figure-eight, so we quickly removed his training wheels, to the neighbor's astonishment. But he did great! I remember enjoying watching him ride when I realized he hadn't stopped to use the bathroom in while. When I made him stop for my examination, I found that not only was he wet, but he was chaffed all the way to his ankles because he had been wet for *so long*. He had just kept racing. "Did you see me, Mom?!"

> Christine (age nine) while peeling apples: "Mom, I am okay. But how do I get blood out of the apple crisp?"

But he wouldn't use the toilet.

As he neared his fourth birthday, I had admitted that the books were right. It had to be his choice, and I would never be able to change that…which was what made me think of "reverse psychology." Moms can be creative!

I put some Cheerios in the toilet and went to get him. I told him, "I bet you can*NOT* sink those Cheerios."

Suddenly, he *wanted* to use the toilet.

Done. No reward needed. He would come ask for Cheerios on his own, not to eat but for target practice.

But what I didn't see coming was when he came to me hours later and said, "Mom, I bet you can*NOT* get me some ice cream!"

He learned my methods of reverse psychology much faster than he learned potty training! But I could have given him ten gallons of ice cream with cherries on top—because I was elated he kept his pants dry for a day almost two years into the project!

Hang in there! I have never met a sixteen-year-old who can do flippy dives but not sink the Cheerios. The light at the end is in sight; it might just be a long, wet tunnel.

God bless,

Terri

Our Turn to Listen

Dear Lindsey,

When my oldest was two, I played the saxophone in a praise band for an evening church service of singing. We didn't practice during the week, which meant we arrived an hour early and worked to be ready. I always brought my son along, and he played with cars or crayons in the pews, waiting for the hour before the service began.

One night when Chris was traveling, Casey was playing quietly and still had crayons out after the service had begun. The pastor was sharing a story he was familiar with, so I tried to draw his attention

> When a friend sits in my car and sees chicken nuggets and Cheerios, I always want to say, "You should have seen it BEFORE I cleaned it!"

away from his toys, "Did you hear what he is teaching? Do you remember that story? I wonder what happens next."

Casey looked up at me with those adorable two-year-old eyes and puffy cheeks, put a finger to his lips, and said, "Shh, Mom, it's his turn to talk and our turn to listen." He then went back to coloring quietly.

Love,

Terri

> After a (false) fire alarm at church yesterday, my daughter said, "Mom, the alarm didn't seem loud enough to wake people up." (Sorry, Pastor!)

Out of My Mind (with a Brain Tumor) Part 1

Dear Lindsey,

Hearing the story of the ten lepers whom Jesus healed (and only one came back to say "thanks") reminded me to say, "Thank you, Jesus. Thank you for every day, every sunrise, every received smile from my child, every swallow, and every breath." I hope to always live in gratitude, but 2007–2009 marked years for which my "Thank you, Jesus!" gained weight.

As I reminisced in writing this story, many of the emotions came back to me—the tears, the stress, and the gratitude for friends.

Here's the story.…

The Headache Journal, December 2007

The arrows that stuck in my husband's back seemed to attract more arrows from other angles. I felt myself crumbling with stress, and yet, crumbling with guilt for feeling stressed. Didn't I trust that God already had this battle for us?!

To my right, the "friend" who stole our Jeep would be in jail, but the broken trust cut deeply.

At my left, I could see the addiction was destroying everything she had known, yet her blindness made her plow forward, not recognizing the monster sleeping within her hobby.

Behind me, I felt the pressure of those Michigan neighbors whose jobs were tanked with the economy. Their children were yanked from my children's teams, as payments for activities got cut with the family budget.

My headaches began so subtly, it seemed I could assign the cause to anything—and thus, "the headache dance" began. I could blame it on stress, lack of sleep, hormones, too much sugar, not enough sugar, too much fake sugar, caffeine, not enough caffeine, not exercising, wrong exercising, not enough water, not enough vitamins, and the busyness of homeschooling two children while entertaining my two- and four-year-olds *and* adapting to a new house in the boondocks of Michigan. My list of reasons for the headaches was enough to give me one.

The scientist in me eventually began a journal—a simple calendar with a note each day labeling the pain between one and ten. Were headaches really ruling me as much as it seemed? The journal began in December 2007.

The grid told the story: five days in a row of level two pain, spiking to level eight, then a day or two off. Then blindness, followed by a twenty-four-hour migraine. Then bliss. Then a couple days of level four pain, ended by forcing myself to bed at level six. There were some days I couldn't remember what it felt like to be without pain, and other days, when the pain was so distant, I would forget the underlying worry.

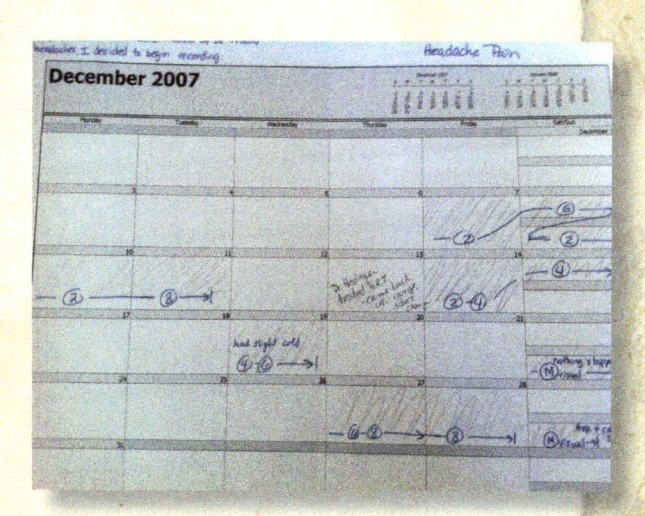

In Hiding, January 2008

To stay focused on others, I don't like to talk about medical conditions. Besides, stating, "I have a headache," only reminded people to tell me about their headaches and did nothing to relieve my pain, much less bring glory to God. Because my husband frequently travels, I knew if he knew my pain, he would feel worse about leaving. But in the hot tub, as I scrunched down trying to heat the nape of my neck, through tears, I put up the white flag of surrender and told Chris I couldn't handle my life.

Aside: *We can't handle it. God does. When we forget, He'll remind us—sometimes gently, sometimes more painfully.*

They were not "headaches"; they were truly "head pains," I told him, not sure what I wanted him to say or do about it.

We wintered in Florida that year, and I had hoped the climate change would bring relief, but it only got worse.

The Florida sunshine became a nuisance; the glare seemed to light a fire in my brain. My vision seemed "off," so I began the headache dance in the medical world:

- "Eighty percent of women complain of headaches with no known cause," the urgent care doctor deflated my hope after I drove myself there for immediate relief once when Chris could stay home with the kids.
- "Eyesight causing headaches is a rarity," said the eye doctor after an extensive exam.
- "Hormonal headaches are something many women just have to deal with post hysterectomy," the OB/GYN told me before changing my HRT prescription.
- "I have taken care of 90 percent of the headaches of which people complain," the chiropractor said caringly; "I really don't know what the deal is."

I waited months and drove hours to see highly recommended holistic specialists.

My prayer journal was filled with prayers for ME.

My Prayers Grew Depressed:

- "God, how can this possibly bring You glory if I am in bed?!"
- "Lord, my two-year-old turned three, and I feel like I am only hiding from him."

- "God, I want to raise my children to be readers, to be disciplined, yet I have virtually locked them inside for months, often in front of a movie so I can lie down with heat on my neck and ice on my forehead. My head can't handle their squabbles, much less lead them biblically through them."

God brought friends who randomly offered to take my kids without truly knowing the extent of my situation. In March, I finally poured out my heart to my friend Donna Ascol and asked for prayer—Matthew 18:19 in action.

Under Pressure…Flying

A flight to Atlanta and then a subsequent flight to Canada that April put me over the top. I was sure my head would burst from the pressure changes; I prayed I would lose consciousness.

Wow. Tears flow today—just in remembrance of trying to keep my world turning that year. My responsibilities didn't stop, and I didn't call, "Mayday!" because it felt like we all have headaches or some other issue we have to push through. However, I promised myself to continue the medical search for a solution, once we returned to our regular doctors in Michigan at the end of April.

In the meantime, a noise began in my head. I researched "ringing in the ears" on the mighty online doctor, who of course told me there was no cure.

The "ringing" turned into a chain saw: a grinding—daily. Sometimes it was louder, sometimes quieter, and sometimes silent. I never noticed it starting, so it must have been gradual (or I was too distracted by head pains). But I never noticed when it stopped either. It just came and went, and eventually, I would become aware of its presence or lack thereof. "Grrrrrrrrr" oscillated between a whisper and a scream in my right ear.

After a brain MRI that month, the general practitioner in Michigan let me know there was a "meningioma on the left side. They're harmless; you may have had it since you were a child, but since you seem symptomatic, you should see a neuro."

The neurosurgeon was not much older than I and had apparently seen more brain MRIs than the general practitioner because she told me the tumor was actually on my *right* side.

"Is *that* why I have this noise in my ear?!" I blurted, for the first time telling a doctor about the noise because I hadn't wanted to mention it to the family doctor; I was surely toying with the psych ward already.

"No," she said confidently. "Your headaches are not related to this thing either. This kind of tumor can come and go in people." (I remembered my dad had had a water cyst found on his brain after a fall a few years back. They said it was not related to the fall, had been there since he was born, and would be until he died. I assumed this was similar.)

"I wouldn't worry about it. Come back in a few months, and we'll do another MRI to make sure it's not growing."

I went home depressed, yet not surprised. I knew the chances of finding the cause were slim. I was hopeful, however, because a new hormone replacement was lessening the headaches, and the ear noise had virtually disappeared by summer.

Melanoma

My older brother had been diagnosed with a rare colorless melanoma (dangerous skin cancer) that winter. After several surgeries, they were able to get clear boundaries. (Thank you, God!)

"Siblings are the most at risk," he warned me. Of course, it reminded me that I had been meaning to get that spot on my leg checked. The dermatologist said it looked fine but wanted to biopsy a different one. Diagnosis: atypical premelanoma. All clear. But when I went back to the general practitioner to have the stitches removed, I asked him about the other spot on my leg that still had my attention. He said, "If it's worrying you, let's take it."

Diagnosis: basal cell skin cancer. (I use the term *cancer* lightly, since it is not the dangerous kind.)

"I must admit," the general practitioner said, "I really agreed with the dermatologist that it didn't look like anything."

He removed several more spots between June and August that year.

Each time I had the stitches removed, the wound would pop open within a day. The lack of healing revealed a pharmacy error. Apparently, my hormone replacement prescription had changed dispensers and been halved, but they forgot to mention to me that I was supposed to take double. The lack of estrogen meant lack of healing (along with other symptoms) until we figured out the solution.

Choking, September 2008

On the way home from an Ohio soccer tournament, I choked on coffee. I know. Who chokes on pure liquid? Me, that's who! I poured hot liquid directly into my lungs…and then coughed and sputtered until Chris almost pulled the car off the highway to try to save me. It felt like more and more often, things were going "down the wrong pipe"!

We had friends over for a cookout on Labor Day. I was thrilled it lined up to a day without a headache, but unfortunately, laughing was painful. As the day continued, I felt like something was wrong in my lungs. My whole midsection hurt. It's funny how I didn't like to talk about medical issues, and the Lord kept having me in places where it was impossible to hide. I couldn't breathe without pain. Laughing—not. I spoke shallowly, with much effort. I finally took aside my friend, Susie Hallstrand, an RN and lifesaver many times over, and told her what was wrong. She did an assessment and decided it was maybe not holiday-emergency-room material, but I should see a doctor the following day.

Is this what it's like getting old? I lamented as my calendar kept filling with doctor appointments: skin, head, eyes, hormones.…*blech!* Back to the family doctor, who named the chest condition something like sore muscles, usually following severe coughing, like pneumonia.

"Or choking?" I asked.

"Sure, that would do it," he said, and I recalled my wrong-pipe incidents that must have led to my painful breathing.

Health Insurance Decline

My insurance company went bankrupt. (*It wasn't my fault! Really!* At least not yet.) As I applied for more insurance, I was turned down. What? Healthy me? Water-drinking, exercising, prayerful *me?!*

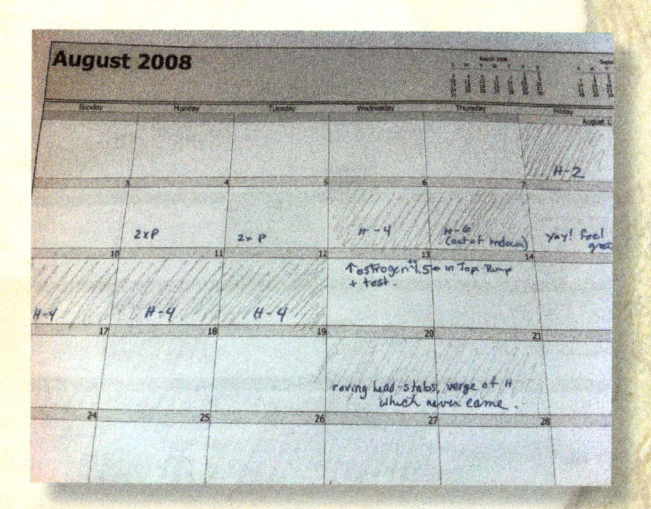

Reason: Skin cancer? Breathing issues? Headaches? What?!

The insurance quote got my attention: "impending brain surgery."

I had never seen or heard those words before, so I really thought there was an error. That week, I happened to be talking to my Florida friend Laurie Woodward, who practically begged me to go back for another MRI, despite how I was resisting it. Really, I had all these other problems to deal with; who has time to go spend thousands of dollars on another MRI to check something that they said was not dangerous or related to these other issues at hand anyway?!

I scheduled an MRI for September 6, 2008, a Saturday, knowing my doctor would be on vacation until September 22, the date of my follow-up appointment.

Like the *Brady Bunch* episodes in Hawaii with the totem pole guy and tarantula,[39] **TO BE CONTINUED…**

Love,

Terri

Out of My Mind (with a Brain Tumor) Part II

Compassion is showing our scars to those with open wounds. —Dr. Gary Hallquist

Dear Lindsey,

In my last letter, I gave Part I to this story. I originally hesitated to share this brain tumor journey: Was I afraid of dwelling in the past? Was I afraid I would scare readers into getting themselves checked for brain tumors? Or was it that my heart ached for so many people still in their "Holland," with worse problems, bigger tumors, cancer in multiple family members, unrelenting back pain, life-changing car accidents, addictions, etc.? A friend reminded me that suffering is not a competition. If showing our scars can be helpful to those with open wounds, then sharing the past is celebrating God's victories. So I continue to write:

When we last left the story, my insurance application had been rejected unless I would get another brain MRI.

September 6, 2008

I had the MRI early in the morning. I "checked off the box" so I could get the new insurance. The diagnostic center gave me the normal line about how I would hear from my doctor within two weeks to review the results. I knew from booking this appointment that the neurosurgeon was on vacation that week, so my follow-up appointment to review the MRI was scheduled for September 22. I was not worried, just like she had told me not to be at my previous appointment months earlier.

The following week, the caller ID revealed the hospital's number on a phone call. The kind woman told me that they needed to get another scan for clarity.

"I am flying to Salt Lake City in the morning," I told her, and we booked a time for the following Monday and ended our call. I figured my brain must have moved during its photo shoot and blurred their view. It's hard to hold still for forty-five minutes—even if your head *is* clamped.

The phone rang again within minutes. "I spoke with your doctor, and she said you should not get on the plane."

"Is something wrong?" The dumb question escaped my mouth as my nerves escalated, realizing they had called the doctor on vacation. Obviously, something was wrong.

"No, we just need a better view. It is actually not an MRI, but a VRI we will be taking," she said as if that was a logical answer to my panicked question.

"So why can't I fly? Is it the plane pressure? I am supposed to leave at 10:00 a.m."

"Well, you could come in at 7:00 a.m., and if the radiologist clears you, you could be out in plenty of time to make your plane."

The following morning, I went back on the cold table into the tube. It screamed a sound similar to the old dot-matrix printer, seemingly through a microphone directly into my ears. Halfway through the test, the young (and obviously naïve) technician started my IV as normal and asked,

"So how long have you known about this?"

Known about what?! went through my head, but I played it cool: "A while," I said, not sure if we were talking about the same thing.

"Can they operate?" she asked, curious.

Oh…my…word. Am I in a Twilight Zone? Did I miss a phone call somewhere? Last I had heard, this kind of tumor is common and no big deal.…"Uh, I don't know yet. I think that's why I'm here." My heart began to race as my mind wandered in what-ifs, but outwardly I was calm.

She asked:

"Is it cancer?"

"I hope not," I said quickly, as if the speed of my answer would bat that chance away.

"Well, you must be scared," she said as she rolled the table with me on it back into the tube.

I lay on the hard, skinny table surrounded by my own cocoon for the second twenty to thirty minutes of the test. I thanked God that the technician was talking to me and not to some little old lady who didn't know my God of peace. I knew the tech wasn't supposed to talk to me like that, but regardless, the cat was out of the bag!

The radiologist released me, I guess, because I made the plane to Salt Lake City…with a headache.

In Salt Lake, we met with close friends and business partners. I told a small few, trying not to initiate panic but asking for prayer and still hoping it would all blow over.

The following Monday, September 22, I saw the neurosurgeon, and she was less jovial than our first meeting months before.

"Your tumor has grown over 50 percent. This is a much more serious situation than I originally thought. It is compressing one of the two main veins to the brain. You probably have heard of the jugular to which it connects. If it continues to grow at this pace, it is life threatening. It is unclear, but it looks like it is close to pushing your right brain to the left, which will cause seizures, so this is becoming an urgent situation. I wouldn't touch it with a ten-foot pole. I am sending you to a specialist a few hours south of here. I assume surgery is your only option. We made you an appointment for next Monday. Bring your husband. You will want him with you."

She handed me two-by-three-foot films to hand-carry to the specialist neurosurgeon in the Detroit area. It felt like the entire office staff was looking at me with a "poor girl" glance as I walked out, but it was probably just in my head. ("Just in my head" began a whirlwind of puns, humor which Chris and I enjoyed to relieve the weight of the situation.)

I got to the car, dumfounded. Opening the humongous envelope that held the films and spreading them across the steering wheel, I could see a lot of gray matter, like any picture of a brain, except one big difference: the white, oblong golf ball on the side. It looked big for my small brain. I searched for my name and date to be sure they were really pictures of *my* brain.

As I drove home, my mind was silent. The chatter of "things to do today" was gone. The bother of the other drivers wasn't registering on my new Richter scale.

Really? This could be it?! *The finish line is sooner than I thought?*

But…my "dash"?!

I remembered hearing Lou Holtz read the poem "The Dash" about the symbol on a tombstone between the birth date and the death date. The dash represented what was done with the life during the time on earth.[40]

My dash may be done?! But I was going to make a difference in this world; I was going to raise my kids to be difference-makers; I was going to spread the gospel: I was going to…

I drove past an abortion clinic, and I was reminded of how many in there didn't have a chance to even start their dash. *Life is not fair. I don't deserve more than they.*

What would I do differently? Ironically, that week I had just read the account of Hezekiah in 2 Kings 20, where Hezekiah was granted another fifteen years of life after he'd been told he was dying. *What would I do now if God chose to continue my dash?*

In my quiet car that day, my priorities aligned, as if seeing a ghost of Christmas future and being pleased. What?! *Pleased?* Yes, pleased. I did not think about where I could have been in the workplace had I only held on to my position in engineering. I didn't think of patents I could have owned or promotions I might have possessed. I realized more than ever that I was blessed to have invested the time of my dash (so far) into being a mom and wife and encouraging other moms and wives. I recognized the *gift* my husband had given me in my being a stay-at-home mom! If God's plan was that I would never speak again, I had no regrets of missed words with my children. I wish that for every woman who chooses to be a stay-at-home mom! If it were all over…

I had no regrets.

I called Chris to let him know the doctor's news, and by the time I arrived home thirty minutes later, he had a dozen coral roses on the kitchen counter, accompanied by his warm embrace.

As the week progressed toward the appointment with the specialist neurosurgeon, my quiet times with the Lord progressed in depth. It is always during storms, when I seek the Son most.

Chris and I kept our secret, trying to protect our children, then ages eleven, eight, four, and three, from fear. The night before the next neurosurgeon appointment, we decided to tell our parents of the impending days.

I had difficulty spitting the words out to my mother and father in Colorado, imagining they would feel helpless being 1,300 miles away and fighting their own medical battles.

My mother immediately reacted as if packing her suitcase: "We will leave within the hour and drive all night."

I was barely able to keep her from hanging up the phone to pack, so I could tell them it was just a doctor's appointment and that I would let them know if indeed surgery was scheduled.

Skull-Base Neurosurgeon, September 29

"The fast growth rate of the tumor tells us it is likely *not* cancer; less than a 4 percent chance."

The appointment gained speed as the skull-base-meningioma specialist went through the options of treatment. "The brain surgery where the child is outside playing later in the day as seen in some commercial is not an option. The size of the tumor exceeds the limits of our noninvasive radiation treatments. Waiting longer to see how the tumor acts [if it would shrink] is getting to a dangerous point, and we have zero data of a tumor that has ever grown at this rate and then stopped. In view of what lies ahead for you, if you have always wanted to go to Hawaii or something, now is a good time to go."

I had never had to endure such a speech, and yet it continued.

"At your age and health, your body will handle the surgery well. However, due to the proximity to the vein, I don't know that we will be able to get it all. I will use scissors so small that the tips can only be seen under magnification, but if even one cell is left, the tumor will grow back. Regular MRIs will hopefully allow us to catch it small enough to use a radiation 'knife' or other noninvasive options next time."

He laid out a plan for future surgeries and radiation treatments dependent on my age at the time of diagnosis and size and growth rate of the tumor.

This diagnosis did not look like it was ending... ever.

His informatory speech continued with how he would enter the cranial cavity (my head!) by cutting a football shaped piece, extract the tumor, and then create a seal to replace the missing skull. The location of the tumor seemed to him far enough from the ear to be able to avoid hearing damage, but it looked like it was directly on the nerves of my mouth; one nick of a nerve would cause permanent paralysis and inability to use my mouth, so he would have a feeding tube team standing by for insertion.

"Is this why I have been choking?" I asked, grimly.

"The location could definitely cause swallowing problems."

He continued to talk about the tumor's location, also pressing on the main vein, as he gave us an anatomy lesson of the sinus vein and its relation to the body.

"I will not get close to touching that vein. I will get every cell I can—as long as it is not touching that vein. If it is nicked, bad things happen."

My heart sank, knowing the tumor was visibly pushing on the vein in the MRI.

Chris excused himself, and I noticed that he, too, was going green in the face.

His absence didn't stop the doctor's progression.

"It is a two-part surgery. The first is done by a vascular surgeon, who will go through an artery in your leg all the way to your brain, to put a 'super glue' (for lack of a better word) into the tumor, to stave off bleeding. This presurgery often avoids the need of a blood transfusion. The second surgery is by my team, the following day. The head surgeon here [no pun intended] will want to be involved, due to the nature of your case, so we will schedule a day for both of us, although I am hoping only one will be needed.

"You will be our only patient for the day. This second surgery will take between two and perhaps fourteen hours. You will be in ICU one night after the arterial procedure, then one or two more nights of ICU after the brain surgery, and three to five days in a regular room. It usually takes two or three months to feel 80 percent healed and a year before patients feel 100 percent."

It had been so long since I'd felt 100 percent that a year didn't seem like a long wait.

"So do you think this will take care of my headaches?" I asked, hoping he would give me a different answer than the last neurosurgeon.

"It's hard to say, but the location of your headaches does not look related to where this tumor is. Unfortunately, I hate to say, but sometimes it can make headaches worse."

I held the tears until Chris and I were alone in the car.

"So let me get this straight:

- If I leave the tumor alone, its growth will likely lead to seizures, paralyze me, and end in death.

- If I have surgery, there is a chance of paralysis or death.

- If I go through the two surgeries and a week in the hospital, and *if* I survive and happen to get myself back without paralysis, the chances are high that I will not feel any better than I have for a year, and I may even feel worse.

- And this is likely not the last time to have to go through all this."

The surgeries were scheduled for October 14 and 15.

As I called my friends, it felt like I was dropping a bomb on each one. I hated to make the call, and yet, I found, through their tears, that the love of Christ in our friendships was shining. When talking with my friend Tracey Avereyn, I was the one who broke down. Through tears, I tried to master the language of cry-talking. I said, "I know that all things work together for good, but is it sinful that I dread this *so* much?!"

Being a sister in Christ, she didn't hesitate to sharpen as iron sharpens iron: "Terri, even Christ went to Gethsemane." In other words, even Christ asked that the cup be taken from Him, but yet He conceded to God's will being done.

The Son of God does not shine so bright as when our world is in its darkest state.

I knew Jesus had been through worse.

TO BE CONTINUED...

Love,

Terri

"When we are young, we learn. When we get experience, we understand."
—my dad

The noise in the dryer was a rock in my son's pocket. Seeking the rock led me to the pack of gum before it had melted. Thank God for the rock.

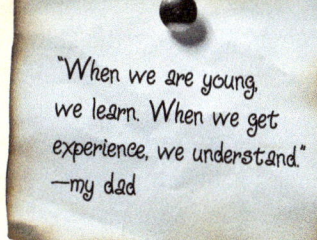

Out of My Mind (with a Brain Tumor) Part III

Dear Lindsey,

In some ways, 2008 seems like yesterday, but as I recall my history, it seems like a whole different lifetime. As I said in parts I and II of this letter, headaches led to MRIs, which revealed a tumor. Although the tumor seemed unrelated to the location of the pain, its speed of growth required surgical removal. When it rains it pours, and so did other "unrelated" health issues—skin cancer, a noise in my ear, and swallowing problems which led to coughing issues—but the brain surgery took priority.

My story continues…

The Two Weeks

For the two weeks before surgery, anxiety woke me daily before my alarm. My 5:00 a.m. quiet times would finish with the Lord's arms around me like a warm blanket on a frosty morning. (Thanks, Alice Doan, a woman from our church, for praying that would happen.)

I was already scheduled to speak in Phoenix, Arizona, and Louisville, Kentucky, those two weekends. I know anyone would have understood if I had decided to cancel due to impending brain surgery, but what happened in those two weeks was a wonderful alignment of priorities.

"What is important now?" dominated my thinking.

If I truly had only two weeks left to live, what would I do? The song "Live Like You Were Dying" talks about going skydiving, Rocky Mountain climbing, and bull riding,[41] but none of that came to mind.

Although I think the chances of handicapping my voice were greater than the chance of death (the surgeon had said he wouldn't come close to the life-threatening vein), it brought the urgency of life to a head, as well as the momentousness of the ability to use my voice. I wanted to live my life on purpose, and I felt like my message to the stadiums those two weekends *was* my purpose, or I would never have planned to be away from my children, even before the diagnosis.

Each weekend, I changed my originally planned speech and told of the upcoming surgery and the heaven that awaited for those who have faith in Jesus Christ—whether the finish line would be October 15 or any time before or after.

During this time, the news of a fatal car accident jarred me to remember that we are all dying. *Every* day is a day that may be the end of our "dash," and priorities should be lived as such, impending surgery or not.

Telling the Kids

The moment I dreaded had arrived: We needed to tell the kids. We knew we had one promise we could make: not "Mom will be okay," not "It will be just like always," but "God is in control."

Pride of being a mother is a difficult thing to fight. Feeling the heavy weight of responsibility, yet keeping perspective that if God chooses, it will be relinquished in a moment, can only be accomplished by surrender. I surrendered (again) that I was not the one taking care of my children; God was. If He chose for me to reach my finish line during brain surgery, my children would still be in His care.

True surrender is the most humble act. I would have told you I surrendered when I was led to Christ at the age of thirteen. Again, a deeper surrender occurred when I "lost control" (which of course was never mine to begin with!) during infertility challenges. I have often surrendered during my battles with pride. But I had never before completely surrendered to the thought that the world would just keep turning in my absence. After a funeral and a passage of time, hearts who may have missed me would heal, and life would continue as it was…without me. The church would find another musician; friends would get back to laughing; business would grow. I am the proverbial drop in the ocean—God's ocean. Removing me was not a big deal. I suppose that is the humility with which we should live at all times, but nothing brought this to realization like a life-threatening storm.

We told the kids the good news: they would get to stay with friends. And then we told them the bad news. Chris grimly went through the recovery information and the risks, and we prayed as a family. Within ten seconds of the word *amen*, Nathaniel (age eight) said, "Can I tell you about the *Scooby Doo* movie now?!"

I know his comment frustrated my husband who wanted more concern, but the child's words were a little note from Above: the kids would be fine.

To the Hospital

After a party for my daughter's fifth birthday the day before, I wrote a little post on a blog my brother Tim had set up to give friends and family updates during my surgery. (The blog has since been deleted—after we printed it—because it wasn't renewed. There were thousands of prayers and comments in the ten days that blog was active. I felt surrounded by loved ones near and far.

I had indescribable peace as we made the two-hour trek to the hospital. I was no longer preparing a basket with pitch and hyssop (from my "Are You a Basket Case?" letter), but like baby Moses, I was riding inside, waiting to see where the Lord would have the water take me. I decided everyone's prayers were like a river on which I floated. So many prayers were said for the surgery, I bet Chris could have performed it!…But I opted for the surgeons instead.

I believe *peace* comes from knowing that in all outcomes: **God is in control.** My thoughts at the time, while reading *Trusting God* by Jerry Bridges, were:

- **God is in control** if I am healed completely.
- **God is still in control** if I have nerve damage and live my life handicapped. (Ask Joni Eareckson Tada if she agrees.)
- **God is still in control** if I have reached my finish line; it would be heaven. Heaven is the finish line, no matter what happens to my today.

First Surgery and a Friend's Call, October 14

The first surgery on October 14 went better than planned; the arterial scope revealed there was no need for embolization to stave bleeding…answered prayer! Because of that, I was able to stay in a regular room and have one less night of ICU.

That night, while lying flat in bed as directed, I received a call from a friend who could hardly speak as she cried, "I don't know if I know how to pray, but I just need to know, Terri, if I pray for you tonight, will God save you?"

Seeing her in her humble state, asking of the Lord for possibly the first time, I replied, "I don't know if He will save me here, but I know if you pray to Him tonight, He will save *you* for eternity."

She and I prayed together on the phone from my hospital bed, as I felt her come to the knowledge of what it means to be a sinner who is completely forgiven and saved by Christ.

Chris and my brother Tim visited with me before heading to their hotel, and I waited for the morning. I glowed with the joy that only comes from knowing another soul will live for eternity.

Today's the Day, October 15

The morning of the surgery, I sat up in bed and posted a favorite hymn on the surgery blog:

"Day by day and with each passing moment

Strength I find to meet my trials here

Trusting in my Father's wise bestowment

I've no cause for worry or for fear."[42]

When rolling my bed to surgery that morning, one of the medical students said to me, "I can't believe you have such peace about this!"

It was ironic that this guy, who was probably used to trying to calm people's nerves, was trying to figure out my lack of nerves. I quoted a favorite saying: "I need not worry about tomorrow; God is already there." I knew I was in my proverbial "basket floating down the river"—two IVs, arterial lines, tubes coming out of every angle, and all the rest. Like baby Moses, I was secured by God's plan, waiting to wake up between two and fourteen hours later to see either Chris or Christ—completely surrendered to His will. Oh, how I pray I live that way out of the hospital bed!

Post-Surgery News

I guess the fifteenth was quite an exciting day full of drama, according to the surgery blog, which I was able to read weeks later.

123

The Summary:
- The tumor was surrounded by a sheath, which protected any nerves from being touched. No nerves to my mouth were damaged!
- The tumor had "fingers" that went into my right ear, so, unpredicted by the MRI's view, several bones from my ear were "eaten through" and were removed. In one of my few memories of recovery, the brain surgeon motioned *"Yes!"* with a clenched fist when I reacted positively to noise in that ear. Although hearing was lost for several weeks due to swelling, the nerves were not severed, and hearing was restored by four months post-op.
- The surgery went as well as it possibly could. I stayed in ICU only one night and a regular room one night—and then went home! (I stayed longer for an emergency appendectomy a year later.) Although I have virtually no memory of that week, my husband tells me that I was in a lot of pain, and he was sure I would get meds in a more timely fashion in our house. (He cholerically took over.) Friends stayed with me 24/7 for ten days post-op, giving me medication and stabilization from falling. I learned what it means to serve one another in love. I only wish I could erase some of those shower moments from their memories. (Yecch!)
- Although unable to get what the medical world calls "clear boundaries," due to the tumor's proximity to the main vein, the brain surgeon had confidence he got all he could see through his microscope. This has been confirmed by years of clear MRIs. (Praise God!)
- I found out a couple of years after the surgery (probably because my memory of the events was tainted) that there had been a twenty-four-hour prayer chain during October 14–15, 2008. Apparently, all through the night, every fifteen minutes, people had signed up to pray—on the phone with one another—in Michigan, Florida, Phoenix, Salt Lake, Louisville, and elsewhere. Wow. I learned what it means to be part of the body of Christ.
- The headaches, the swallowing problem, and the ear noise were all healed. By January 2009, Chris was forgetting I was recovering and asked me to go snowmobiling! (I said no and reminded him the helmet would not feel good.) Really, less than three months after surgery, I felt better than I had felt in years. Chris said, "I feel like I got my wife back!" I still stand in awe.
- I never before 2008 thanked God for a reflex like swallowing, but it still comes to mind. I learned that I have taken the body's involuntary reflexes for granted.

When Bad Turns to Good:

I feel extra-blessed if I get a glimpse of God's plan when something I perceived as bad turns through a winding trail to be better for me after all.

- My brother's melanoma was such bad news, but if he had not called me, I might not have had the skin exams—which led to my recognizing the skin-healing problem. I cannot imagine I would have survived brain surgery lacking the ability to heal.
- The rejection from the insurance company was a disappointment the day I received it; however, that rejection (along with Laurie Woodward's encouragement) is what spurred me to get the second MRI. God's thoughts are always higher than my own, and He meant it for my good (Isaiah 55:8).
- The physical pain was bad, but it was good because it forced the solution. Without the substantial physical pain, I might not have sought help as fervently, and the tumor would have grown inoperable. (It reminds me of sin! But I will save that for another letter.)
- I believe my friend (who prayed on the phone with me from my hospital bed) was changed for eternity—heaven instead of hell—when my illness caused her to humbly reach for a Savior (John 3:16). There is no greater joy for those who ask.

Whether or not we see the good coming from bad, we can be thankful for the struggles because they promise to give us perseverance, character, and hope (Romans 5:3–5) and increase our pain tolerance too!

During a horrible storm that was tossing the fishermen's boat in the billowing waves, Jesus said, "Peace, be still," and the winds and waves obeyed His command (Mark 4:35–41).

The old hymn says, "The winds and waves still know His voice who ruled them while He dwelt below."[43]

Although He may not remove you from the water, may you experience His peace as He calms the storm within.

In Christ,

Terri (See below for Frequently Asked Questions)

FAQs:

1. ***Will the tumor come back?*** I was told there is a documented average 20 percent chance of return when they get clear boundaries around the tumor's location. Since they did not get clear boundaries, the chances would normally be considered greater, but my surgeon was very confident that he got every cell, so any return would be due to its ripe environment for growth. After the five-year mark, the chances of its return decreased significantly. At this book's latest

printing, I have been cleared for over 15 years! When I thought of stopping the regular scans due to the exorbitant cost, Chris said, "What else could I want to spend money on? I only have one wife; I want you to keep having the scan every year."

2. *Were there residual effects on me?* Yes. The biggest effect is that I am more grateful for pain-free days than ever. The other effects are minimal in comparison, and I don't like to talk about medical things. ☺

3. *Do you still have headaches?* Yes. I am back to "normal." I have even spoken in front of a crowd—lights and all—with a migraine. To me, it is a testimony of increased pain tolerance. The occasional headache now comes as a blessing, reminding me of my past as "the leper" who came back (and continues) to say thank you.

4. *Was the brain tumor caused by cell phone use?* I have read probably too much information on this topic. Although evidence is still questionable, it can't hurt to hold cell phones far from the ear and limit children from holding phones to their heads. (Their skulls are softer, and the radiation has been measured much further into their brains.)

5. *Do you think your healing was a miracle?* I don't feel worthy of the term *miracle*, considering the miracle of a virgin's birth or raising of a Man from the dead. However, I don't take from God that He provided answers that the doctors were unable to predict. *To God be all the glory.*

Tumor Humor: Out of My Mind (with a Brain Tumor) Part IV

Dear Lindsey,

After letters I, II, and III of my brain surgery story's drama, I have to tell you how much laughing Chris and I did before, during, and especially after the surgery was successful. If you are in the middle of a health battle, I hope humor can help take weight off. I never mean to offend.

God knew we needed a laugh to ease the nerves as I checked into the hospital on October 14. After fasting fifteen hours, driving two hours to the hospital, going through the extensive check-in process, having IVs started, and then sitting for hours waiting for the arterial scope the day before brain surgery, it was a good time for some distraction! Chris and I began going through text messages on our phones that we had not had time to read the week before. Many of them had scriptural references, so I had a Bible (NKJV) ready to look up the verses, while Chris read both of our phones.

A friend texted: Psalm 71:21. So I looked it up: "You shall increase my greatness and comfort me on every side."

Another was Romans 15:13: "Now may the God of hope fill you with all joy and peace in believing, that you may abound in hope by the power of the Holy Spirit."

We continued, one after another, until one stopped me in my tracks: Our Florida pastor, Tom Ascol, had sent Chris a text referring to Romans 8:32, so I anxiously read the verse from my Bible,

"…He was led as a sheep to the slaughter; and as a lamb before its shearer is silent, so He opened not His mouth."

What?! I read it again silently.

"...He was led as a sheep to the slaughter; and as a lamb before its shearer is silent, so He opened not His mouth."

A lamb to a shearer? Right before they shave part of my head? A sheep to slaughter? Before brain surgery? Why would Tom send such a note today? I don't think that's a funny joke. Tom has a fantastic sense of humor, but his timing is really off on this one; there must be a mistake.

"What was that reference again?" I asked, hoping Chris had read the reference wrong or something.

"Eight thirty-two," Chris said.

Yep, that's where I was, and I couldn't believe it was true.

"Romans?" Chris asked, hoping he was getting his friend Tom out of hot water.

Ohhhhh! I thankfully realized that I was in the wrong book: I was reading Acts 8:32.

(I laugh now when I see that I pridefully assigned blame everywhere but to myself. I laugh harder to think I would have believed Pastor Tom would *ever* text such a verse. Ha!)

We went on to read Romans 8:32, "He that spared not His own Son, but delivered Him up for us all, how shall He not with Him also freely give us all things?"

Much better.

We called the Ascols in Florida right then from the hospital bed to share the story. We laughed and praised God for the humor to relieve the stress.

In previous letters, I alluded to some of the lingo we used on purpose during this time. It's more fun to laugh than cry, and these colloquialisms have different meanings for brain surgery patients:

- I gave the doctors a piece of my mind.

- I am no longer in my right mind.

- I am a little out of my mind.

- They had to take a piece of my brain, so I would be back on level with my husband.

- I need to have my head examined.

- I thought something was wrong, but it was all in my head.

- I needed to have the head surgeon present (from Part II).

- This brings the urgency of life to a head (from Part III—did you catch it?).

- I think I have a screw loose. (My skull was "put back together" with titanium screws.)

- And my friend Jen texted, "Your blog will really help some people, but don't let that 'go to your head.'" Love!

In fun,

Terri

Thanks Again

by Terri Brady
(from Luke 17)

Ten lepers were healed
By Christ's words that day.
He said, "You are new,"
And sent them away.
They danced and they sang
With their limbs now anew.
Showed friends their new health
And all they could do
One returned thanks,
The others took for granted;
But Jesus gave freely
His gifts not recanted.
Lord, help me to be
The one of the ten
Who thinks to come back
and say, "thank you," again.

May God bless you with much, and may you bless Him with thanks.

Terri

"Mom, I Need the Bug Swatter Thing."

Dear Lindsey,

After bedtime, Casey (age three) was at the top of the stairs yelling for me. When I arrived, he said, "Can you please get me the bug swatter thing? There are two bugs: one here [by the gate] and one in your room."

I said, "What were you doing in my room? You're supposed to be in bed."

His eyes got *huge* as if to wonder how I knew he was in my room. Finally he answered, "I was looking to see if you had any bugs."

With love,

Terri

The day after watching Super Bowl commercials:
Waitress: "What can I get you?"
Nate (age four): "I'll have a Bud Light."

When I explained to Christine (age seven) that a meter is almost the same size as a yard, she asked, "How do you know how big someone's yard is?"

"Mom! Something's wrong! My belly just said, 'Oink.'"
—my seven-year-old

Me to my six-year-old: "J.R., do you know what size shoe you wear?"
J.R.: "I think it's twelve and a half feet."

Wet Light Fixtures and Oatmeal Kisses

Dear Lindsey,

Tuesday, I left three children for a few hours in the morning while I went to see a friend who was dealing with news of the unexpected loss of her father.

When I returned, a Brady crime scene was under way. Water was pouring out of the light canister in the ceiling of the first floor. I walked past to find the two male culprits adorned with wet hair and towels, full of sorrys as they explained conflicting versions of how the splashing out of the second-floor bathtub had caused the problem.

Walking toward the stairs to go examine the Jacuzzi tub access, I glanced at my Christmas nativity scene in the front foyer and noticed socks. Ever since the decorations went up this year, this particular nativity scene has had Mary, Joseph, Jesus, and a pair of socks, a lollipop, a jack ball, half of a cookie, a piece of cheese, or whatever else had been in the child's hand when he walked by and set it there. Tuesday, it was socks…again.

> After a seven-day trip with my husband without me, my daughter came home with the same braid in her hair from her departure….I feel needed.

Walking down the second floor hall to get to my room where the water war had begun, I had to complete the obstacle course of a "store," with signs bearing, "ART FOR SALE!" as my eight-year-old hustled next to me, telling me all about how she was saving to buy a goldfish now (*Maybe I should have waited on the puppy?*) and asking would I *please* buy her art this time?

Thoughts spun in my head, whirling from the shock of the early phone call's bad news, to the extent of water damage to the light, to *How could this much mess be created in such a short time?* (a question frequently in my thoughts). Yet the question *When will my house ever stay clean?!* was not fully formed before I remembered my favorite poem, which fantastically reframes my thinking every time:

I found it originally with that famous author "unknown."

"Wet Oatmeal Kisses"

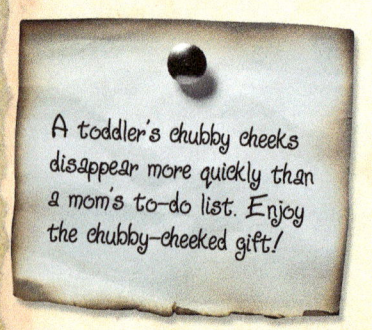

The baby is teething.
The children are crying
Your husband just called and said, "Eat dinner without me."

One of these days you'll explode and shout to all the kids,
"Why don't you just grow up and act your age!" And they will....

Or, "You guys get outside and find something to do—without hurting each other. And don't slam the door!" And they don't.

You'll straighten their bedrooms until it's all neat and tidy, toys displayed on the shelf, hangers in the closet, animals caged. You'll yell, "Now I want it to stay this way!" And it will....

You will prepare a perfect dinner with a salad that hasn't had all the olives picked out and a cake with no finger traces in the icing, and you'll say, "Now this is a meal for company." And you will eat it alone....

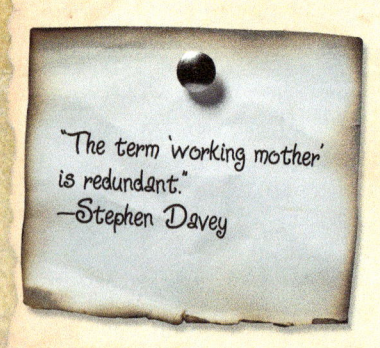

You'll yell, "I want complete privacy on the phone. No screaming. Do you hear me?" And no one will answer.

No more plastic tablecloths stained. No more dandelion bouquets. No more iron-on patches. No more wet, knotted shoelaces, muddy boots, or rubber bands for ponytails.

Imagine a lipstick with a point! No babysitter for New Year's Eve. Washing clothes only once a week. No PTA meetings or silly school plays where your child is a tree. No car pools, blaring stereos, or forgotten lunch money.

No more Christmas presents made of library paste and toothpicks. No wet oatmeal kisses. No more tooth fairy. No more giggles in the dark, scraped knees to kiss, or sticky fingers to wash.

Only a voice asking — "Why don't you grow up?"
And a silent echo — "I did."[44]

—Author Unknown

A toddler's chubby cheeks disappear more quickly than a mom's to-do list. Enjoy the chubby-cheeked gift!

"The term 'working mother' is redundant."
—Stephen Davey

Children are the anchors that hold a mother to life.
—Sophocles

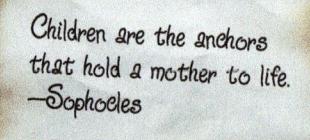

May your day be filled with more wet oatmeal kisses than wet light fixtures—and proper perspective when both occur.

God bless,

Terri

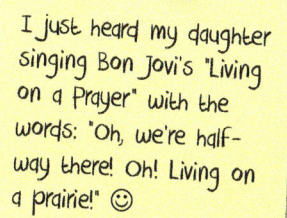

> *I just heard my daughter singing Bon Jovi's "Living on a Prayer" with the words: "Oh, we're halfway there! Oh! Living on a prairie!"* ☺

Coyotes and Jesus

Dear Lindsey,

Years ago, at the soccer field with my older boys, I heard this exchange between my daughter, then four, and another parent on the sidelines:

> Parent: "What's your name, little girl?"
>
> Daughter: "Christine, after Jesus and Daddy."
>
> Parent: "Oh! Well what's your daddy's name?"
>
> Daughter: "D-A-D!" ☺

Once when my children were young, I took them up onto the back deck after sunset so we could behold the amazing sky of stars God had displayed that night. As the breeze swept across the surrounding woods, the leaves sang, and animals scurried. In the distance, an ominous howling reminded us of the nocturnal hunts occurring, while we simply enjoyed a peaceful moment as a family.

> *"I love it when the milk is going to go rotten on my birthday!"*
> —Christine (age seven)

"I'm sc-scaaaared," my three-year-old Christine said, crawling into my lap. "I don't want the coyotes to get us."

I was amused, since the coyotes were clearly far away, and we were clearly thirty feet off the ground on the upper deck. Before I could console her, Nathaniel (then six) said, "It's okay, Christine."

His tone was so comforting. I smiled at the irony that he was probably the one who had introduced her fear, but I was thrilled that this time he was being kind.

> After the Polynesian show in Hawaii, where a man put fire in his mouth, J.R. (age six) said, "It smelled like real fire, but it couldn't be his real tongue because he didn't cry."

Then he continued in the same joyful tone: *"You believe in Jesus, so you will go to heaven when the coyotes are done eating you."* ☺

The talk of Jesus in our house is evident in the language of my children. But a few months ago, our pastor here in North Carolina, Stephen Davey, asked a key question that I thought I would bring home to my kids, then fourteen, eleven, eight, and six. *"On a scale of one to ten, with ten being 100 percent sure, how sure are you of what would happen to you if you died today?"*

I thought this heaven/hell question would be an easy one for the Brady Bunch in my house. We have read the Bible together and attended church, have sung hymns and prayed together; but their answers took my pride right to where it should be—in the Lord's hands. They didn't know.

I am not here for a theological discussion, but I *am* here as a mother who loves the Lord and wants the same for my children. Do you know the answer to the question, on a scale of one to ten? Do your children? Shouldn't we ask? Their answers that morning were eye-opening; I realized I had improvements to make in my most important job. Feeling tugged in so many directions, I tend to look for perfection, but I know that my children's answers to that question shook my attention forward. I love to serve at church, in business, and in the community, but my priority is teaching my kids the answers to crucial questions in life.

Love you, girlfriend!

Terri

When We Don't See a Purpose

Be kind, for everyone you meet is fighting a hard battle. —John Watson (aka Ian MacLaren)

Dear Lindsey,

My friend and pastor, Tom Ascol, was struck by lightning in 2008 and lived to tell about it. The aftermath was difficult, to say the least. No visible signs were on his body, but on the inside, the electricity and its effects continued to surge. Unable to sleep due to the excess energy, he lay awake for days on end; even eating was a tremendous struggle. Noise and light were amplified to him to such a degree that he felt most comfortable alone in a house with lights out and shades pulled. Although his internal life was changed in a split-second flash, onlookers could simply see a man.

His family decided to go ahead with an already-planned vacation the next week, thinking that getting him out of town might give him more solitude. One problem: the Atlanta airport for the connecting flight.

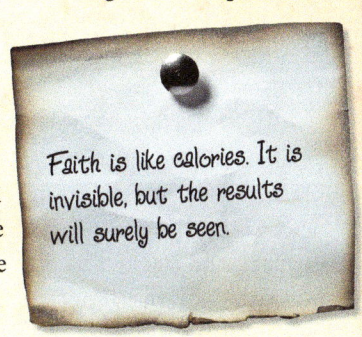

> Faith is like calories. It is invisible, but the results will surely be seen.

People raced in every direction, while my friend shuffled his feet, trying to make his body do what it used to do. Loudspeaker announcements made him wince; lights made him want to hide. His wife stood by him as they walked slowly. She saw people huff and puff, frustrated at her husband that he wasn't going as fast as they seemed to think he should. No one could know what kind of life-threatening week he'd had. No one could understand why he looked "normal" but acted differently. No one seemed to care.

Struggles are like cockroaches.

- For every one we see out in the open, there are hundreds hiding in the walls.

- Everyone has a battle with them in their house (for cockroaches, at least south of the Mason Dixon; for struggles, everywhere), and no one likes to admit it.

- They have a purpose under heaven; although under heaven, we don't always see a purpose.

- There are none in heaven! (For struggles, see Isaiah 65; for cockroaches, Book of Opinions 1:1.)

I am not a fan of cockroaches. Go ahead; start a website: "CockroachesAgainstTerriBrady.com." Fine by me. You can tell me they are harmless all you want, but they give me the creeps. I have seriously wondered why God would put such creatures on this earth with me.

> *Struggles are like cockroaches. For every one we see out in the open, there are hundreds hiding in the walls.*

But they served a purpose under heaven once, and I realized, once again, that my ways are not His ways and my thoughts are not His thoughts (Isaiah 55:8).

It began with a twenty-seven-year-old friend of mine who was diagnosed with terminal stage-four colon cancer. Doctors estimated that six months of life remained for this beautiful, seemingly healthy young mother of two. Diana never put a period where God had put a comma. She had surgery and then fought the fight, yet humbly submitted to God's will throughout her struggle.

Our mutual friend Sheri let me in on a secret: Diana had never seen the Atlantic Ocean. Immediately, we booked flights from Colorado for Diana to join Sheri and me at the Florida beach. The trip was amazingly blessed. We went from blood-sweating prayer, to tearful questions, to girlfriend laughs. Diana caught her first fish off of my dock, and a mother manatee and her twin babies surfaced to look at her as if she were Snow White. I was beginning to call her the "animal whisperer," but apparently, she had that effect on cockroaches, too!

We took the beach chairs out of the storage bags, and cockroaches jumped to the ground, scurrying every which way. My oldest son tried to bury them, and a seagull dived and caught one before our eyes. Yay! One cockroach down, and a seagull had eaten something besides my sandwich!

After the excitement seemed over, Sheri, Diana, and I lined up our chairs to watch the surf come to the sand in the waves' motion. A pod of dolphins appeared in the distance, as if continuing Snow White's show.

Suddenly, I felt that unmistakable crawling feeling: a three-inch cockroach was *on my leg*! He ascended my inner calf, making me scream like a hyena. It really is not like me, but I screeeeeeamed! I jumped up, trying to shake him off. The more I shook, the tighter the varmint held on. I began to run….in circles….around Sheri and Diana's row of chairs, now forming words, "Get it off! Get it off! Get it off!" while visions of it crawling up between my legs haunted my head.

I stopped in front of Sheri's chair and asked, "Is it gone?" pointing to the back of my leg where I couldn't bear to look!

"No," she calmly said.

"Can you pleeeease get it *off*?!" I asked, fully expecting her to flick it to the ground.

Sheri shook her head and wrinkled her eyebrows. "Um…water?" in a "duh!" kind of tone. She shooed me with her hand, motioning for me to go into the January ocean.

I didn't hesitate. I screamed my way to the ocean and sat in the waves, watching my nemesis float away—to be scooped up by a seagull.

That's when I noticed. Diana was laughing. She wasn't giggling or snickering; she was *laughing*. She grabbed her waist, which was still sore from surgery, but she couldn't stop her hysterical laughter. It was then that I noticed that the beach was not empty but *full* of people in front of whom I had just made myself a complete *fool!* It made me laugh—louder! The three of us got such a side-splitting, gut-wrenching laugh out of it that joy seemed to shower upon our threesome. For a moment, it took away the weight of the cancer, the prognosis, the battle, and the death sentence that loomed over our friend's head and in each of our hearts.

The mini-vacation lasted only two days, but every hour or so, it seemed, one of us would bring up the cockroach word or the cockroach dance (La Cucaracha!), and we would begin laughing all over again.

When I dropped Diana at the airport, I wondered what God had planned for her. I wept at the pain of her struggle. I hate to see someone struggle! I see no earthly reason for it! I prayed in tears.

Days later, I got a text from Diana, "La cucaracha!!" and I laughed out loud. The "cockroach" word became our inside joke that fueled our ability to laugh during a horrible time.

Diana well surpassed the doctors' six-month prediction, but when July arrived, it became evident that her body was indeed shutting down as the cancer was winning the battle for her life, at age twenty-eight.

Believing in Jesus Christ as her Savior, she knew she would be going to heaven, so at one point, she asked me to describe for her what heaven would be like. I told her all that I could remember (mostly from Isaiah 65 and Revelation 21):

- "There will be no more tears!

- No sound of crying anywhere!

- No darkness of night, but no sun required because God's glory will light the whole thing!

- More beautifully decorated with gold than could be described!

- Jesus is there and has a room prepared for you, and I hope it's near mine!

- Diana, you will be given a new heavenly body, with no more pain!"

As I spoke through the verses I could recall, I looked forward to going there myself, and I certainly looked forward to it for Diana's pain-riddled body.

"Learn to appreciate what you have before time makes you appreciate what you had."
—Jackie Lewis

Texts became one-sided as I sent Bible verses and prayers in her direction and got none in return due to her decline.

In September, she was told it looked like only weeks were left. My aunt died that month, so I flew to Colorado for her funeral, and I was able to stop in and see Diana. From her feeble body, her inner strength still shone outwardly when she said, "I don't understand, but I trust Him" (Proverbs 3:5). We prayed that she would be spared, and yet we wanted God's will to be done. What a joy to pray with a believer!

In October, her husband texted me that hospice said they thought she was within hours of death.

I decided to text one last thing.

Then I stopped myself. I was concerned that my humor would offend her husband, and it's the last thing I would want to do. I erased the text and prayed.

After some time, the thought wouldn't leave my mind, so I followed through and texted her husband, "Whisper in her ear, 'There are no cockroaches in heaven.'"

Message sent.

I got a text back from her husband that said Diana had reacted to my words with a full-face smile, the first response to anything they had seen in four days!

God had used the cockroaches! What smiles they delivered—even in her last days on this earth.

Two days later, she went to live with her King Jesus forever, in her new body with no more tears, no more pain, no more night, and, I believe, no more cockroaches.

Struggles are like cockroaches. Many times we have no earthly idea why they are here, but we can trust that God has heavenly ideas.

"Every circumstance that touches my life has first been filtered through His fingers of love."[45]
—Nancy DeMoss

To recap, struggles and cockroaches have a lot in common:

- For every struggle we see in the open, there are probably hundreds more in private, so be kind.

- Everyone has struggles; you are not alone.

- Struggles have a purpose, although under heaven, we don't always see one.

- There is no suffering in heaven! Amen.

May you trust Him with your struggles—the ones in the middle of the floor and the ones behind the walls: the lightning strikes, the health problems, the marriage problems, the overwhelming debt, and the cockroaches. If He can use cockroaches to bring smiles to a dying woman, how much more can He do with you, His loving child, as He holds you throughout these days and into the bright, really, really bright skies ahead?! Keep holding on!

Blessings,

Terri

"God is always on plan A—ALWAYS."
—Anne Winters

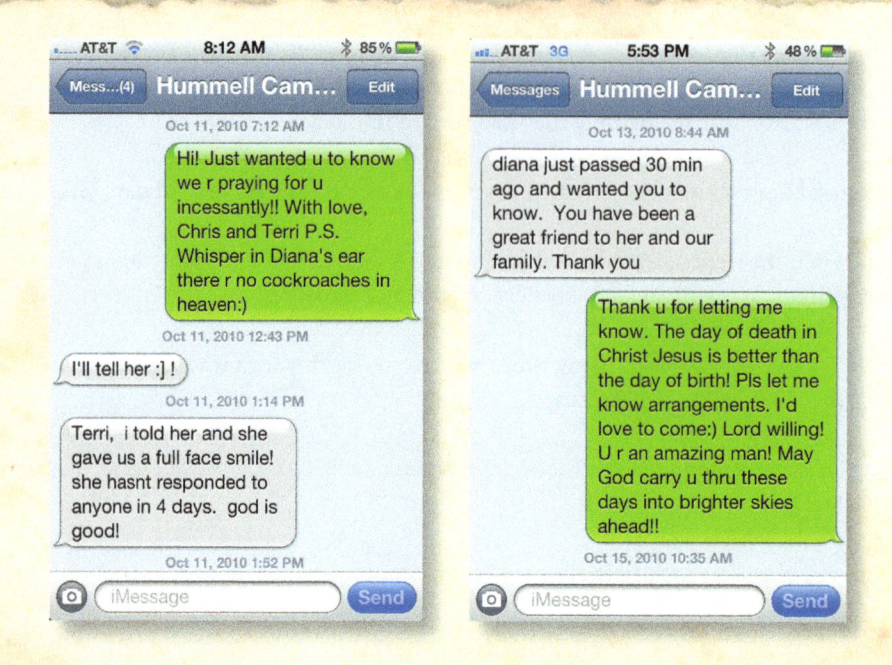

"Never put a period where God has put a comma." —Dr. Robert Smith Jr.

Crucify Him! (the Song)

Good Friday

Dear Lindsey,

Music somehow reaches the core of my being. A certain song will command movement and make a workout more intense; another tune will force a smile to take over my countenance; yet other combinations of notes slow my pulse and restore me.

"I wrote this song yesterday; I think this is the piece we have needed for our Good Friday service," Dr. Gary Hallquist, the pastor of music ministry of our church, said a little over a year ago. His music writing amazes me.

Our Good Friday "Service of the Shadows" is a choral and orchestral production centered around Scripture reading, depicting the last days of Christ before crucifixion. The lighting changes to darkness slowly throughout the musical evening, ending the service in complete darkness and silence, as if the Light of the World were extinguished. On Sunday morning, the service begins with the last song of the Good Friday service, performed in the dark, and then the lights come up—into full brightness to celebrate the Resurrection.

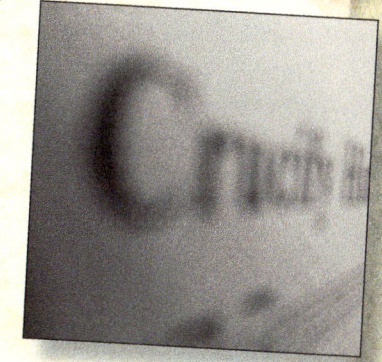

At the Service of the Shadows, singing "There Is a Fountain" or "Oh Precious Savior" leaves the listeners and singers in wonder and awe of Christ. But Gary's song called "Crucify Him!" stirs different emotions. I didn't want to sing it.

The orchestra leads the introduction with dissonance. Conflicting notes that don't yield "happy" build on top of one another, creating suspense like the theme from *Jaws*. The listener is transported back in time to the day that Pontius Pilate, the Roman governor of Judea, asked the crowd, "What do you want me to do with Jesus?"

"Crucify Him!" is almost shouted in bass tones in a syncopated rhythm that is woven throughout the piece. The shout begins on the first beat of the measure, but then it changes—beat two, or the second half of four, as if a crowd is sporadically shouting their opinions, yet so musical in chorus. The orchestra echoes the rhythm, with the bass instruments randomly repeating it while the choir is singing other melodies, like an underlying hatred in the world.

I hate singing, "Crucify Him!" The words pierce my heart, yet I know singing it creates the emotions for the service that must have been there the day the chief priests and officers were shouting it to the Roman prefect (John 19:6).

> The men sections come in full force, singing the words of Pilate in powerfully ominous bass tones: **"Whom do you want me to release to you?"**
>
> The choir women answer as if they are the crowd of Jewish leaders in front of Pilate, **"Give us Barabbas!"**
>
> **"What do you want with Jesus, your king?"** Pilate (the choir men) asks.

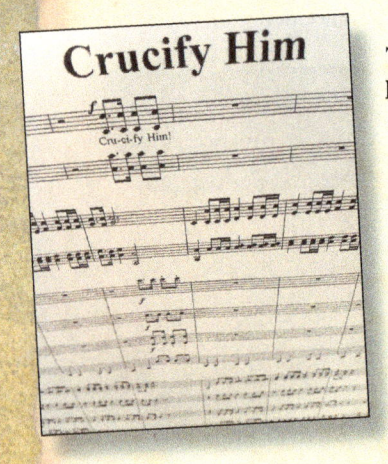

The crowd (choir women) interrupts with the answer, "**We have no king but Caesar. We want Him put to death! His blood be on us and our children!**"

What…an…angry…crowd. I cannot imagine the emotional overcast that day.

Do I have to sing and pretend to be that?! I would *never* scream, "Crucify Him!" If I were there, how could I possibly say that I would rather have Pilate release a criminal and kill the Son of God instead? Barabbas was known for robbery, which in those days often meant terrorism or bloody insurrection (Mark 15:7). I would *never* have chosen to release him, knowing that with my words, I could have voted for Pilate to release Jesus, a man who never sinned, instead!

Do you ever have these thoughts?

- "How could those leaders act like that? Wasn't a crowd just yelling, 'Hosanna! Blessed is He who comes in the name of the Lord!' last Sunday?" (John 12).

- "How could Peter, one of the disciples, say he didn't even know Jesus, when just hours before, Jesus had washed his very feet with His own hands?" (John 18:17).

- What kind of man is Pilate, that he would allow a crowd to make the decision for his conviction?

- "I would *never* yell, 'Crucify Him!' I would never want to free a bad guy instead. I would *never* say I didn't know Jesus. I would never be like that."

But I can never say "never."

The best way to avoid accidentally expressing a judgmental opinion of a friend is to not have one.

When I judgmentally thought, *That's disgusting*, looking at someone dressed differently, adorned with things I would not have near my body, and walking in an unattractive way, I was not loving.

When I had to talk myself back into emotional control when the flight attendant gave me a hard time about "FAA regulations" (which must not have existed on the three previous flights that day!), I was not seeing her as Jesus.

When I received a negative e-mail, how much did I want to return the negative with a kiss of betrayal?

"Crucify Him!" I was shouting with each thought, each emotion, each lack of love.

If I am not for Him, I am against Him (John 3:18). I shout "Hosanna!" in church, and by the end of the week, or sometimes even that same day, I have denied Him three times.

> I cannot say "never."
>
> Barabbas was guilty.
>
> Jesus was innocent.
>
> Barabbas lived. And on that first Good Friday, Jesus died in his place.

I have been Barabbas.

I am guilty; Jesus died in my place.

Maybe Pilate represents all those men of power who lack the courage of their own convictions. He thought Jesus was innocent (John 18:38; 19:4, 6) yet followed the crowd.

I have been Pilate.

Peter may stand for those who have been there: felt their guilt, know their need for a Savior, and yet hide it under the pressure of the "in" crowd, a friend, or a spouse.

I have been Peter.

As we remember the day that Jesus was crucified, may we lay our own lives aside and live for Him. "Greater love has no one than this, than to lay down one's life for his friends" (John 15:13, NKJV).

May God give you grace to believe in Jesus and crown Him as Savior and Lord today.

In love,

Terri

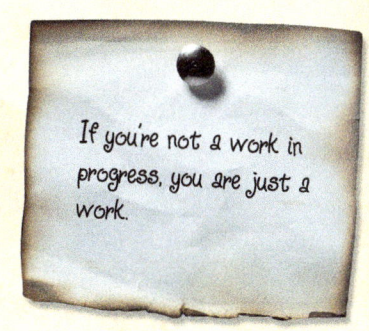

If you're not a work in progress, you are just a work.

Blessings That Stick

Dear Lindsey,

I am in Guatemala!

"I don't think I have ever smiled so much and spoken so little," my friend Susie Hallstrand said. I guess that's what happens when you dive into playing with children of an orphanage in a land of a foreign tongue. Jen Korte, a Michigan soccer mom friend of mine, extended her heart beyond imagination all the way to children in Guatemala. She has visited Dorie's Promise, a private orphanage in Guatemala City, many times and invited Susie, Tracey, Dianne, and me to go to the land for our hearts to grow. Forever Changed International (FCI) is a charity that not only supports the orphanage, but along with the organization Believe Guatemala, also aids the poverty-stricken within Guatemala City.

Today was our first full day, and many apprehensions were cleared while the chains of our hearts loosened. We are staying in an adjoining house that sleeps twenty. We are with other Americans from Oregon, New York, New Jersey, Michigan, and California.

Life is a mission trip.

After attending church in Spanish, where the Holy Spirit transcended cultural differences, we took the orphans to the park where the laugh of a three-year-old child (whom I was teasing with tickling on the swing) was a universal language. Those children went back to their house, which runs like a daycare; but it runs twenty-four hours a day, seven days a week, and is much more permanent now that international adoption is closed.

Next, our team of volunteers left the grounds to go to one of the many ghettos in Guatemala City. As we drove, Joel Juarez, the angel who hosted and translated for us for the week, explained that ghettos begin when a group of approximately one hundred simply sets up a camp on city property. The sheer numbers prevent authorities from removing them. "They begin with a hundred people and some cardboard boxes," Joel continued, pointing to a relatively new cardboard ghetto as we drove past. "Over time, the people add more and more and eventually end up with something like the ghetto we will visit today."

When the bus finally stopped at the appointed place, we were immediately surrounded by children, excited to see *gringos* (slang for white people) bringing gifts. I began to wish they would realize the gifts were not because of the color of my skin but because of the God who created it.

Jen handed me stickers she had brought from the States, and I began giving them to the children, while she handed out other gifts. We walked through the streets, followed by a crowd who loved "the day the gringos come" (first Sunday of the month for this location). We carried stuffed animals, food baskets, and two piñatas to end our day with a party. I overheard Tracey ask Joel, "How do you say, 'God loves you,' in Spanish?"

Perfect! I thought. *I can tell these children God loves them while I hand out stickers.*

I continued handing out stickers. "*¡Que Dios te bendiga!*" ("God bless you!") I said as I pressed a sticker onto each hand and looked deeply into their eyes.

> The greatest weight loss program is the one in which we recognize that the world does not rest on our shoulders.

I hate poverty.

Seeing ominous clouds coming in our direction, I pictured what these homes would look like when the storm hit. This ghetto was more established than the ones we passed, so walls were made of cement or built into the side of the mountain, but I could picture the noise of rain pounding on the tin roofs, leaking through, while ten people huddled in the middle with one square foot per person. Each "building" was smaller than my eight-year-old's room, and I never saw a bathroom. The "kitchen" was a shelf of pots and pans next to the bed, but I never saw food, except once: corn hung from the ceiling to dry. The woman grew corn on her own in "free land" a mile and a valley away where she planted and hauled it back to dry, in order to grind it for flour to make tortillas on the open fire in the "hallway." When we walked by, she had tortillas cooking under her close watch, hoping to sell them later for profit.

We continued our walk, stopping at houses to meet residents and ended in the park for play and piñatas. Word got out that I had *stampas*, and children flocked to me. I practiced my Spanish, asking if they wanted the princess sticker or the flower. "¡Que Dios te bendiga!" I said with each gift.

A sticker brought delight to these kids who probably wondered when or if the next meal would come. One baby had a "crib," which was a blanket tied to the ceiling "beams" with rope as a hammock above an adult bed. My legs ached at the hill climbing and uneven steps OSHA would never approve.

I still hate poverty.

In my mind, I raced to solve the issues....*A new roof for that one? Cement floors so the dirt doesn't wash away under that leaky roof? Running water?*

How did they get here? Education? If only they knew a better way. Do they know the Hiding Place where they can go? Do they know that heaven will be better?

Thoughts pounded, and children enjoyed our presence.

Better is one day in heaven than a thousand on earth, I thought. I am grateful for the volunteers here. "Well done, my good and faithful servant!" will surely be heard by Joel, Jen, and the hearts that surround the work to make this place better for these four hundred or more children in this one ghetto alone.

But I look forward to heaven for those residents. One minute of eternity will erase all hunger pangs from a life here.

I prayed for the children while I watched them race for candy, a temporary joy amid the struggle called life.

Suddenly, a group of young teen girls approached me, interrupting my thoughts. The four giggled incessantly, as though from my American neighborhood. They all looked on in anticipation while they egged each other to ask a question. Finally, one stepped up and asked:

"Cómo se dice 'Que dios te bendiga' en inglés?" ("How do you say 'Que dios te bendiga' in English?")

"God bless you," I answered. They each repeated it slowly, practicing, trying to cement it to memory to be retrieved later. I was overjoyed by their approach.

I hope that when the gringos are gone tonight—as the rain pours outside—those children will remember His name above all else. "Yo creo tambien." ("I believe [in Jesus] too!") one woman told me at our departure.

37,000 orphans in Guatemala.
Only 33 adoptions last year.
No orphans of God.

May God bless those born into poverty to be rich in Spirit,

Terri

"Call Mom!"

Dear Lindsey,

J.R. (age six), who is smart as a whip, is just learning phone manners. I try to teach my kids to answer our home phone, "Hello, Brady residence; this is _____," the way I was taught as a child.

He has even memorized my ten-digit phone number. He called me once last week, and it went like this:

Me: "Hello?"

J.R.: "Brady residence; this is J.R. Who is this?"

Me: "This is Mom. You called me, so you don't say the 'Brady residence' part, okay?"

I have been playing the piano for Casey's school choir one day a week. Since I homeschool the younger three (ages eleven, eight, and six), they are left by themselves—a new thing now that the fourteen-year-old goes to school. I guess because it is new that they are home without Casey, they feel the need to call me—even when Chris is home! Last Monday, my phone had seven missed calls from the "Brady residence" in the one hour I was gone!

So Friday, when I left for a short appointment, I gave more explicit instructions. "I am only going for one hour. Please do not make my phone ring, unless it is your last call before dialing 911."

I was gone ten minutes when my phone rang.

Me: "Hello?"

J.R.: "Hi, Mom, what time is it?"

> My son (age six) called me on my cell phone today and said, "Brady residence; this is J.R. Who is this?"

> This morning: Me: "J.R., go brush your teeth, so we can start school." J.R.: "Mom, I just brushed them yesterday!"

Me: "Three o'clock."

J.R. "Okay, thanks." Click.

I said a quiet prayer, thanking God he hadn't called 911...yet.

Love,

Terri

> "Dad's Black Ops Jeep, to a guy, is like chocolate to a girl."
> —Casey (age fifteen)

Canine Quandary

Dear Lindsey,

You are familiar with the success principle:

1. *Define:* what you want to accomplish, Lord willing.

2. *Learn:* from those who have accomplished it.

3. *Do:* what they did. Apply their principles so you are not wandering around unguided in a desert.

There is one area of the Brady home life right now that *really* needs to apply those three steps. Her name is Delilah, and she is our seven-month-old Havanese puppy. In order to start the process of learning, I sent out a letter to my neighborhood association. I was almost laughing by the time I was done typing it, so I thought I would share it with you:

Letters to Lindsey

Hi! I just went for a lovely evening walk through our neighborhood and couldn't help but notice the large quantity of dogs and how well behaved they are. One sat quietly at its owner's command while we walked by; another expressed aggressive interest but stayed in his yard (presumably encouraged by an invisible fence); others were walking on the opposite roadside but acted as though they barely noticed my puppy and me, despite the fact that my puppy was strangling herself trying to get to them.

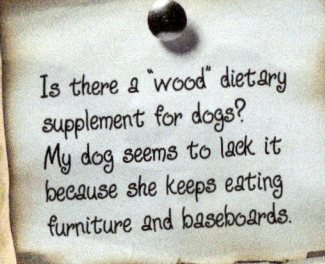

How did you do it?!

Is there a "wood" dietary supplement for dogs? My dog seems to lack it because she keeps eating furniture and baseboards.

My puppy has been through the six-week puppy training at Pet Smart, and it was very helpful; however, there must be more. I have read *Puppies for Dummies*, *No Bad Dogs (Just Bad Owners)*, and *How to Raise a Puppy You Can Live With*…and I can't live with this one yet. Please let me know if you can recommend the best way to get a well-trained dog, with of course, the least amount of time; however, I understand there is a time commitment to excellence in any area.

For entertainment purposes (for those still reading), here are some facts about my seven-month-old Havanese:

- She is carpet-trained. She won't go outside or on the hardwoods, only on the carpet. (Okay, this one is actually getting better, but we have not made it twenty-four hours without incident yet.)

- **She ate the wood on our coffee table last week. Yes, ate.**

- She dug a hole in the wall-to-wall carpet in two places, while there were six people in the house at her beck and call.

- If she gets outside without the leash, she bolts quickly to the neighbor's yard with a vendetta to do her business, as if it is a trick we taught her—despite the fact that since October, we have only taken her to one place to do her business several times a day (and it was NOT the neighbor's yard). SORRY!

- When we use the clicker in the house, she runs to us immediately. If we use the clicker outside, she runs across the street in front of cars or whatever it takes to get away and make us feel foolish trying to get her back.

- **She has eaten through three leashes. Yes, eaten three.**

- She swallowed two of the medical magnets that were to decrease the pain level in my son's knee. Everything came out all right.

    Okay, I tell you all the bad, but there are equal amounts of cuteness that almost make up for the thousands of dollars in doctor bills from her hip surgery that was necessary because, apparently, one of the times she jumped down the hardwood stairs put her femur on the outside of her hip socket. Now I like to say I taught her a trick called "Walk on three legs," but she is actually starting to use the bad leg again—so it's time to train her to be a good dog.

    Thank you for any recommendations you have for trainers or methods I should research. Thank you equally for any encouraging words (and no discouraging words—this is not an ignored or maltreated dog). I am excited to be able to let her one day live outside of her crate and off of a leash in our house, as a trusted member of the family (who doesn't eat the furniture, etc.).

    God bless,
    Terri Brady

So girlfriend, there you have it. I have often wondered where my time goes in a day, but letters like this remind me: my time as a domestic engineer is not my own; there are problems to solve.

I have only had a couple of recommendations of local trainers from the neighbors. One promised that her friend's dog was "a new dog" in one week. I might go with that one and just ask for the new dog.

Love ya!

Terri

"Is it okay to eat plastic?" she (age eight) said, trying to get the plastic off of her lolly pop. I only wish the dog would ask that question.

I just saw a first: a "Bakery for Pets." I am SO glad Chris didn't know you could do that to them.

The trainer said, "Dogs will not wet where they sleep." The Brady dog is extraordinary!

Watching the whale show at Seaworld in Orlando makes me wonder if I am the wrong owner for my dog.

Somehow, it's flattering that my dog is so excited to see me she wets herself—except when she wets my seat in the truck on a long trip.

Delilah (our puppy) ate Chris's walnut desk in the dark this morning. Oh my! Most dogs are afraid of the dark. My dog is amazing!

Seeing the otter show at Seaworld in Orlando made me think I have the wrong pet.

Delilah (our puppy) ate the new carpet for a snack while I worked six feet away. I am tweeting this to see if Chris follows me on Twitter.

Cat Aversion

> I asked my kids' friends, "What is your favorite seafood?" Angelina (age seven) said, "Shrimp." Andrew (age eight) said, "Hush puppies!"

> "I love forgetting because it's so fun when you remember!" —Christine (age nine)

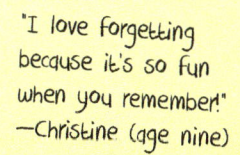

Dear Lindsey,

Sometime near my son's first birthday, he had a deadly allergic reaction to his first taste of milk. Welts decorated the quickly swelling skin, changing the proportions of his facial features to an unrecognizable state. The pitch of his cry ascended higher and higher, as assumably, the windpipe narrowed. Fortunately, Benadryl relieved the scary situation during my debate of calling 911.

Within the next year, the specialists confirmed Nathaniel was indeed allergic to not only milk but also eggs, soy, and beef. The doctors were puzzled since this normally hereditary condition had no previously cited experiences in our family.

The new diagnosis made it difficult to visit restaurants without causing a scene. In the church nursery, I attached a sign to his back which read, "Please do not feed," as I walked away in prayer that he wouldn't accidentally pick up someone else's sippy cup. When we traveled, some establishments were off limits, while others jumped through hoops trying to get the cute little guy something to eat. A decade later, food allergies still shape the social event of eating, often making him feel like an outcast everywhere but in our home.

At age five, Nathaniel went to visit his cousins, who had a new cat. After returning from their house, he begged for a cat. "Please! I love their cat! Their neighbor has kittens! For Freeeee! Our cat could have kittens, and we could sell them! I will take care of it all by myself!"

I then realized that due to the severity of his allergies, I had never mentioned my own less-than-dangerous ones. I thought telling him might make him feel better. "Hey, bud, I may have never told you this, but actually, I am allergic to cats. We will never have a cat in our home."

He raised his eyebrows, and the left side of his upper lip in that unbelieving way and scolded me, "Well, you don't have to *eat* it!"

I hope this brought your God-given smile to your face!

Love,

Terri

> Is there a difference between dots and polka dots? Are there other dance dots?

J.R. (age seven) is lifting weights "to make myself strong enough to carry the blueberries I am going to sell" (once he buys the plants).

City Slicker Farming

Dear Lindsey,

Ever since my first child was two, I have enjoyed taking my kids hand in hand for a morning outing to the Farmers' Market, filling our basket with the fruits and veggies of the season, and finishing our day with a locally made treat such as homemade donuts, turkey sausage, or ice cream.

When Casey was two, he was "helping" me carry a bag of peaches. To my surprise, he wasn't beside me when I looked down to talk to him. I searched the path behind me, as booths and people lined the edges, and I saw smiles on all of the faces. Without a care in the world, Casey had sat down in the dirt in the middle of the crowd, legs sprawled, and decided to have nature's treat. Peach juice ran down his face onto his shirt, clear to his elbows. Onlookers smiled at the scene, but he didn't notice them. He just enjoyed his peach. It's such a fun memory to recall, now that he is fifteen and towering over me!

Yesterday's trip involved my youngest two kids, ages eight and seven. We began in the building section, which held craftsmanship of all kinds. J.R. was particularly excited to see the "boomerang store."

I had taken Christine and J.R. to the Famer's Market in my small car (BMW 3 series convertible). And after our shopping, Christine wanted to buy a fig tree with her allowance money so she could "sell figs." (I love her entrepreneurial spirit!) The ten-dollar price/risk/investment seemed perfect for the teachable moment. I thought about bringing the truck back to transport the tree, but then we realized we could set it at her feet in the convertible, with the top down, and it could stick out the top a little. Have you ever seen a convertible driving down the road with a tree sticking out?

Then, you guessed it; it started to rain. It rained on the just and the unjust alike, and we got soaked. Have you ever seen a convertible driving down the road with the top down in the rain? With a tree sticking out? With children under the tree? I especially had to laugh out loud at the stoplights—which *of course* turned red at our approach—while I sat next to "normal" people in cars, listening to their music, not noticing that the woman next to them was singing in the rain with two kids and a tree sticking out of her car! "Mom! I won't even have to water my tree today!" Christine yelled from the backseat while I continued to sing for fun.

We made it safely home, with my hurricane hair and a fig tree.

This morning, J.R. woke up and immediately asked, "Mom, can you take me to the Farmers' Market today? I want to buy a blueberry plant."

Thanking God for the joys of motherhood today,

Terri

PS: They started their own "save the trees" club. TTC stands for "The Tree Club," and its purpose is to collect money to buy the trees at the Farmers' Market so none of them gets thrown away. One of J.R.'s many titles is "Idea Man: thinker, if other members can't!"

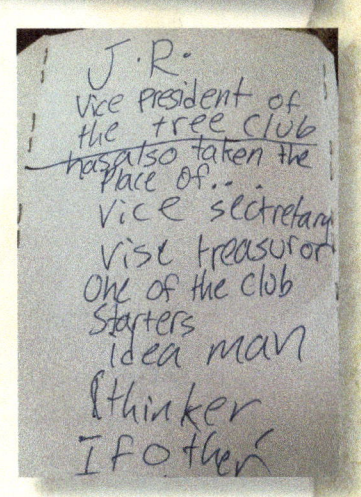

J.R.'s business card

Dampened Impressions, Toddler Style

Dear Lindsey,

Company is coming! The holidays begin! Candy from October 31st still lingers in my kitchen, and I can't believe it's already the next holiday!

My preparations today remind me of a day a couple years ago:

I have had their last name for almost two decades, but trying to make a good impression on my in-laws is still one of my strong desires. I want to make sure they know I am the perfect wife for their perfect son. ☺ They encourage me and tell me nice things all the time, but as a daughter-in-law, I always want to do more for them.

Case in point:

The oven had been hot, preparing the holiday goodies all day. The laundry room was equally hot, as I tried to get all the tasks done before their arrival. I wiped counters and awaited their text: they could be here any minute. All the boxes were checked off—if that last load of laundry could get put away!

The text arrived! "GPS says we'll be there in 10."

I worked to mop that floor one last time and hopefully put on makeup as if I always look "done-up" for their son…but that one last load of laundry was still in the back of my mind. Oh, how I wish I could clone myself for times like this!

Wait?! Isn't that why I had kids? "J.R.?" I yelled up the stairs to see if the last remaining unworking child was within earshot.

"What, Mom?" the five-year-old yelled back down.

> My six-year-old just told me he has a headache in his foot.

"Grammy and Papa will be here in ten minutes. The dryer has your clothes in it. Could you please fold those and put them away?"

"Ten minutes?! Yaaayyy! Sure! I'll put my clothes away!"

A guilty thought crossed my mind. *Is that a lot to ask of a five-year-old? He's folded clothes beside me many times before. The dryer happens to only have his clothes in it, so he'll know where it all goes, right? They don't have to be folded perfectly; they only need to disappear into his drawers, right? Perfect! I have time to get myself ready!* I raced upstairs to the master bath.

"They're here!" the screams began from each of the four children. No question that the white van from Michigan had pulled into the driveway.

Whew, the floor dried in time! I thought as I descended the stairs to the clean kitchen to greet Grammy and Papa. Chris came out of his office; the holiday had begun!

Later that evening, as is tradition (and such a great break for me!), Grammy and Papa headed up the stairs to help the kids to bed. The kids anxiously picked out their favorite books and brushed their teeth, looking forward to their "scratch-backing" time while Grammy and Papa read books. That's when Grammy yelled down:

"Terri? Do you have a leak somewhere?"

A leak? You're kidding me!

I raced upstairs to find that she was baffled why all of J.R.'s pajamas in the dresser were *wet*.

> Am I the only mom who gets in public places with my kids before noticing what they are wearing?!

As I inspected the situation, I found that not only were the pajamas wet, but so were all the underwear, pants, and shirts…that he had put away from the dryer.

"J.R., was the dryer off when you took the things out to put them away?"

"No. You didn't say they had to be dry."

Be thankful you have clothes—even if they are wet.

God bless,

Terri

> My six-year-old has told me he's really afraid of getting "Jack's itch." I think he means "jock itch."

Donating through Dinner, Kick-Starting the Heart

Dear Lindsey,

I love the idea of "required acts of service" for my son's school, but the pressure to do it feels wrong when he's fighting the clock. Couldn't the intent backfire by hardening a teen's heart if he resented being "forced" to serve someone? I have had this thought many times in parenting: when I have forced an apology, forced sharing, forced reading, and forced good action when the child's heart was not in it with me. "If the right action is taught, the heart can follow," I concluded once again, knowing I can teach the action, but only God can change the heart.

This incident began as a school requirement.

Or maybe it began when I went to Guatemala to visit orphans in October.

…Or when we started splitting allowance into giving, saving, and spending jars when he was six.

God knows when the idea began, but a new chapter was written last week when Casey, my fifteen-year-old, was completing his requirement of three hours of "Christian service" due last Friday. In the past he had done lawn work for the less fortunate or volunteered on a soup kitchen team with classmates, but now he was down to the last week and needed to think fast. He asked me if I had any ideas.

My thoughts pelted: *He could make dinner for a neighbor and checkmark his requirement for the grade. He could babysit a friend's kids for free, but that wouldn't help his heart in reaching others in the name of Christ, which is probably the teacher's goal.*

That's when I heard noise outside. Christine, my nine-year-old wannabe philanthropist, who loves the thought of owning a business, had begun another one in the driveway: selling "arts and crafts" that were made from the trash in our garage. She and her neighborhood friend Karsen had decided to raise money for the orphans in Guatemala. She was yelling up and down the street like a town crier: *"Finally! Something to make you feel good about spending money!"* she yelled to an empty street, waving a poster in her hands.

There are less than ten houses between ours and the street's end, so less than ten cars would be passing…probably after 5:00 p.m., and it was only 2:30. J.R. (age seven) sat patiently by the cash box in the wagon, waiting for customers. Another Norman Rockwell scene at the Brady house.

Kind dog walkers (who must have brought their wallets!) bought $4 worth of painted soup cans and cardboard houses.

Christine was elated! She had a goal to raise money to sponsor an orphan for a month ($35 minimum).

That's a lot of decorated trash to sell, I thought.

That's when the idea developed. Casey and I ran with it.

"We could sell dinners to the neighborhood and raise money for the orphans!"

And so it began.

> Things must change inside your house before they'll change outside your house.

Chris, the marketing expert, taught them how to word a flyer that would go out to the neighborhood. "'What's in it for *them*?' is what you want to put first," he said.

The three (Casey, Christine, and J.R.) decided "what's in it for their customers" was:

1. Donating to a good cause

2. Yummy homemade dinner

They worded and reworded the flyer until it looked like this, with the subject line: "Donating through Dinner."

> To all of JP [our neighborhood]: the Brady kids (Casey 15, Christine 9, and J.R. 7) are hosting a fundraiser to earn money for orphans in Guatemala, and would like to offer to make your lives easier by bringing you dinner!
>
> We have made delicious potpies, brownies and cookies, and all you need do is reply with how many potpies you would like. The price is $10 per 9" pie, and for an extra $1, you will also receive 6 cookies/brownies/a mix, of your choice.

Please reply, first come first served!

100% of the profits will go to Forever Changed International, to support Dorie's Promise Orphanage.

Simply answer back with your address and we will bring dinner to you! (all that is required is oven heating).

Thank you for helping us make a difference in the lives of the less fortunate.

The Brady kids!

(P.S. If you have concerns about food allergies, we do too! Just ask!)

(P.P.S. Please hurry and answer before Dad eats all the brownies!)

His dad doesn't know what a pastry blender is (an old joke in our marriage), but Casey made the crusts from scratch (with a little help from me in the rolling) and loaded the meat and veggies into pans, while Christine made brownies, J.R. made cookies, and I stood in awe as supervisor. The kitchen was full of joy, the kind that only comes through serving others. Even the cleanup didn't seem like work.

They had lost themselves.

They sent the flyer through email distribution to our neighborhood that night and headed for bed.

Within fifteen minutes, my email was active: all of the pies were sold. Orders continued into the night, and I thought about announcing they were sold out, but I tried to sit back and let the business owners decide.

The next morning on the way to school, I told Casey all the potpies he had made had been requested and asked what he wanted me to do with the remaining orders.

He was shocked but thrilled.

"So let me get this straight: I worked for four hours, and we can sponsor an orphan for five months?!" he said as he did the math of their proceeds.

"If this rain cancels soccer tonight, I hope we can do more!"

His heart was in it!

Whether it's time or money, the joy of giving can be duplicated in no other way than…giving. Sometimes you act, and the heart follows.

> 19 pot pies: $190
>
> 17 desserts: $17
>
> To an orphan: 5 months
>
> A heart changed: priceless.

Change works silently on the inside before it is ever evident on the outside.

God bless,

Terri

"Whoever refreshes others will be refreshed." (Proverbs 11:25, NIV)

"A person doesn't feel, then act; rather, he acts, then feels. Change actions to change feelings."
—Orrin Woodward

"At the heart of our problems is the problem with our heart." —Chris Brady

Duh, Mom

Dear Lindsey,

Casey, my oldest, was an especially intelligent toddler. At two, he knew our five-digit address, as well as many of the neighbors' addresses. Sometimes his gifted brain may have come across as a smart aleck because he said things so confidently. It was as though he was saying *"Duh!"* to the adult who asked the questions.

Even as a baby, he seemed to have it all figured out. When I would play peekaboo with him, I felt like he was saying, "*I knew you were there.*"

My father often recounts the time he asked two-year-old Casey if he had a fire truck in his hand.

Casey replied, "No, this is the pumper truck, Pop Pop."

While pushing his Hot Wheels on the carpeted family room floor, he regularly made an elaborate scene—usually a traffic jam. One houseguest walked by and, observing the cute display, said, "Are you driving your cars in the city?"

To which Casey replied, "No. There is no engine or steering wheel; I am just pushing them with my hand on the carpet."

Toddlers make me laugh!

Love,

Terri

> "Don't cut your shirt by accident," I said to J.R. (age seven) as he cut a paper he had taped to his costume. He grinned: "Mom, you don't know my skills."

> During a hug: "Mom, why do you have a big nose?"

> Nate (age twelve): "Why 'Thursday-night football'? Don't they know the number of kids in this country who suffer because they can't stay up?!"

> J.R. (age seven): "You know, eight is the perfect age. It opens up everything: bumper cars, no car seat, everything!"

Hold It Down!

Dear Lindsey,

Ha-ha! I remember Dr. Dobson taught that when teaching children verbiage for referring to certain body parts or bodily functions, we should use caution because it will be screamed across the church pews or in the middle of the grocery store or at a grandfather's funeral. With this in mind, we chose carefully how the Brady brood would be referring to the bathroom, saying "#1" and "#2," as they were the least of many evils.

However, when it came to the body part, it seemed strange to give it a code name because the code names I had heard never seemed to soften the sound:

"Mom, my wee-wee hurts!" from across the room didn't leave anyone guessing what was in pain. "Mom, my piggy is sticking out of my underwear!" just doesn't sound like a cleaner thing to discuss in public. Pretty much, the body part is just that: a part of the body, and so we didn't rename it anything special.

When my first son was newly potty-trained, I hadn't put it together yet that boys usually *stand* to use the toilet. Oops! So there were a lot of issues—especially in small stalls of public restrooms. Two of us had to fit in there, and I was usually standing in the front, at the target position of his weapon while he sat. I would often say—with urgency in my voice, trying to avoid getting sprayed—"Hold your penis down! Hold it down!" to get it contained before I got wet.

Once in a public bathroom *full* of ladies, after my two-year-old son had used the bathroom, I took my turn, while he stood in front of me in the same stall. With tremendous urgency in his voice, but *louder* than I have ever said it, he said, "Hold your penis down, Mommy! Hold it down!"

I suddenly felt like the girl in the itsy-bitsy-teeny-weeny-yellow-polka-dot bikini who didn't want to come out of the water. I was afraid to come out of that stall.

I don't think it would have mattered if we had renamed the body part.

I just thought you'd enjoy a laugh!

Love ya,

Terri

> Christine (age eight): "Twelve is the perfect age."
> Nate (age twelve): silence.
> J.R. (age seven): "Yeah, eight and twelve are perfect."

Random Thoughts of a Child

J.R. (age six): "Mom, wouldn't it be weird if we didn't have noses? We wouldn't be able to blow up a balloon."

Dear Lindsey,

I love it when my children say random sentences. They are like little gifts of smiles for me from God. These were so random! I mean, picture a child sitting at the kitchen table coloring, and out pops the thought, "God can see your underwear." So funny! I only wish I had had access to a pen every time, before their funny words slipped my mind. Here are some favorites I remember:

- "If you didn't have lips, you couldn't say *p*; you could only say *t*."

- "I think this is when tornadoes like to come out."

- In a prayer, "Dear God, sorry I sometimes say 'yuk' when the food comes."

- "Are honeymoons fun?"

- "You have to love everyone—even the evilest eighty-year-old lady."

- "Wouldn't it be cool if pigs laid eggs?"

- "Why does everyone want to see Old Faithful? Who cares about volcanoes?"

I hope your day is full of smiles!

Terri

Christine (age seven): "Mom, if I catch a squirrel and teach it to do tricks, can I sell it to earn money?"

"Mom, I brushed my teeth last night, and they weren't even that bad!" —J.R. (age six) in his "Yay me!" voice.

J.R. (age six) on the long ride to Florida: "Mom, I can balance my Frisbee on my nose and my knee."

New word by Christine (age nine): Supposals: things you can imagine to be true (while playing with Legos).

J.R. (still on the long ride to Florida): "Did you know if you color with a highlighter on your body and then go in the dark, you glow?"

Christine (age nine): "God is so cool to create a finger just the right size to scratch that spot inside your ear without hurting anything."

"Mom, I wish I had two powers: invisibility and teleporting. What about you?" —J.R. (age seven)

J.R. (age seven) at lunch today: "When I grow up, I want to be a comedian and then a CIA agent, and then maybe I'll play soccer."

My six-year-old son brought one pair of shoes to Hawaii for the week. Who said they have to match (each other)?

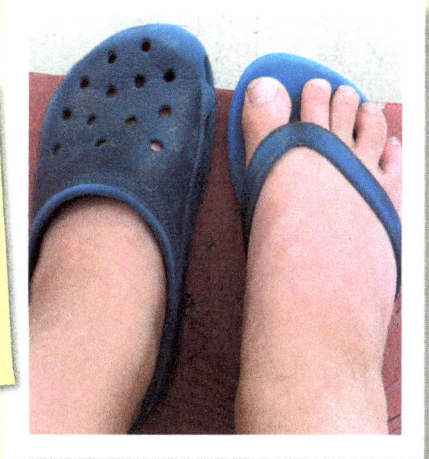

Honesty: Uncovering 10:08s

Dear Lindsey,

In the car one day, I overheard my son, J.R. (age six), say to his older brother: "My heart always hurts *so much* until I say I'm sorry when I need to."

> "God always sees our underwear."
> —my six-year-old

The doctor asked my friend's father, in his dying days, if there was anything he could do to make these days more comfortable. The elderly man replied, "Do you have anything that takes away a guilty conscience?"

My fourteen-year-old emerged from his bedroom one morning, and the first words he uttered to me were "Mom, I'm sorry." When I asked why, he explained, "Last night, when you said I could read until 10:00, I actually read until 10:08 because it was the end of the chapter. I am sorry."

I must confess that as he told me, I *laughed* inside. Ha! Do you know what most teenagers are into these days? Do you know what I did when I was fourteen? (Okay, really, it was *all* my brother!) My son is not perfect; believe me, but "sorry because I stayed up reading"? Really? Is that an offense in the Brady house? Oh sinner! Ha-ha! Next, are you going to overindulge on vegetables?

By the grace of God (seriously!), I did not laugh but told him he was forgiven, and then I entered into that deep thought in which we moms get lost:

> I should tell him: He is acting like a geek, a nerd. This could be painful in front of peers. They could tease him. He needs to know that 10:08 is close enough. I mean, it didn't even inconvenience me.

I then realized that I had somehow changed standards. It was as though I thought 10:08 didn't need an apology because:

> My son just said, "Mom, the cupboard door will be closed, so why do we have to clean inside?" Is he running for political office or what?

A. It didn't inconvenience me.
B. It wasn't bad compared to his peers.
C. There was some good in it. (After all, he was reading, not checking bad websites.)
D. He didn't get caught.

But in the Brady home, honesty isn't the best way; it's the only way. So in our Guidebook, it says that even 10:08 requires an apology. According to Paul David Tripp in *The Age of Opportunity*, our goal as parents of teenagers isn't to build fences in which our kids stay, but to teach principles that they will use to guide creation of their own fences in life.[46] God provided "fences" in the Ten Commandments that are specifically for protecting us. I thank God that my son had his own fences, from Exodus chapter 20, and not the ones I almost botched with my less-than-godly standard.

> "It's amazing how much more difficult it is to say, 'Can you forgive me?' instead of just, 'sorry.'"
> —Nate Brady (age twelve)

It seems to me that the embezzlement of millions—which puts people in jail—begins with stretching the truth about a few pennies. The extramarital affair that tears apart a family starts with one small thought. We judge those who get caught, while we overlook our own offenses as minimal because we were "close enough." The Judge above sees it differently. When my eldest's conscience is wise enough to discern the difference between 10:00 and 10:08 and seek forgiveness for disobeying his mother, he deserves applause.

His mom's thoughts? She is asking forgiveness while she types! And she's praying that God will reveal all the "10:08s" in her own life, so she can eliminate them. If we can hold an honest standard for ourselves and emulate that for our kids, maybe we'd have less embezzlement and fewer extramarital affairs and more men and women deserving to hear, "Well done, My good and faithful servant."

I have heard it said, "There is no softer pillow than a clear conscience," and there's no clear conscience without admitting wrong—and asking forgiveness (Acts 3:19). My six-year-old as well as the elderly man in the examples above knew it. Maybe we each know it deep down—that the little things do matter in the really *big* picture (Hebrews 10:16–17).

Blessings,

Terri

"Repent, then, and turn to God, so that your sins may be wiped out, that times of refreshing may come from the Lord…." (Acts 3:19 NIV)

Letters to Lindsey

"'This is the covenant I will make with them after that time,' says the Lord. 'I will put my laws in their hearts, and I will write them on their minds.' Then he adds: 'Their sins and lawless acts I will remember no more.'" (Hebrews 10:16–17 NIV).

Art Exchange

Dear Lindsey,

I found a note on my desk from my daughter. It read, "Dear Mom, I borrowed some paper but will give some art." As the paper was indeed returned in its promised form, I was pleased and impressed with the variety: paintings and pen drawings, notes and three-dimensional creations came pouring back onto my desk—all from a ream of paper and its cousins: Post-it notes and canvas. Her brothers helped.

The colors were beautiful on the flowers that echoed God's creation. The drawings have improved through the years of her youth, as the once stick figure now has eyes, expressions, and even backgrounds of mirrors or wheat fields. Sometimes the paper comes back as a pleading note, an invitation to a "Be Happy Today Party!" or as a glitter-filled "I'm sorry. I was rong. Will you fergivv me?"

The notes to me, personally, hold a special place in my heart: "MOM WOW!" or "I [heart] Mom," or I especially love the picture of me inside of the world.

"You're the best Mom 'in the world.'"

The love letters to me are equaled only by those that tell of love for her brothers and dad, "The best thing about you is…" or "I love J.R." or "Nate, you are always the laugh-maker that keeps me happy."

As I read her note of borrowing paper and returning art, I saw such a parallel in that

God has given us pages to fill with our art.

As the LIFE book, by Orrin Woodward and my husband says, "Life is a gift from God, while what we do with it is our gift back to Him."[47]

We have 365 pages each year to return to Him with our "art." Unfortunately, I know there are days—no, actually I know there are *years* when I have given back nothing but scribbles, wandering back and forth aimlessly as my pen kept drawing. Other days have gone by as unfulfilled lists: things "to do" that didn't receive my effort. I am trying to push out of memory the pages of life where my day caused pain to others (like the one note I found from one of my children to a sibling that said, "You are stoopid" that I threw away instead of photographing). Some of the days God gave me were wasted because I was too self-absorbed, hiding my art, thinking it was unworthy to share with others.

On occasion, I returned to Him pages of "sorry" and "please" just like my daughter's notes to me.

We can see our own created "art" change from stick figures to colors, to backgrounds and hopefully even a little depth through the years, as we become new creatures. I pray that we create pages of our life with our best effort, not for a blue ribbon on earth or a trophy on TV but for His utmost glory.

God doesn't judge us by our ability to draw, any more than I worry about the spelling on the love notes from my kids. It's the love that matters. All we ever have to be is what He made us. So let's "make art" and do it with excellence, every day. I think He would love a picture of me loving my husband in private and in public. He might enjoy a visual of me listening to or otherwise helping a stranger. His joy must abound in our thank-you notes. He would love to see that in the depths of my heart, I love *Him* and think He is worthy of awe.

When Jesus was asked what the two most important commandments were, He replied, "Love the Lord your God with all your heart, all your soul and all your mind. And the second is like it: love your neighbor as yourself" (see Matthew 22:37-40 and Mark 12:30-31). So it seems that the pages of our lives that God Himself would enjoy the most are the same notes that were my favorites from my daughter's drawings: "I love my brother," and "I love You."

May this day of your life be a masterpiece for His name's sake.

Love,

Terri

Letters to Lindsey

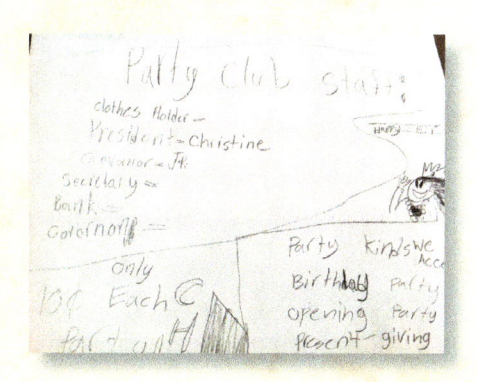

171

LETTERS TO LINDSEY

172

Short, Sweet Prayer

Dear Lindsey,

My four-year-old once prayed, "Jesus, you are such a great guy. Amen."

Amen,

Terri

"Jesus said, 'Let the children alone, and do not hinder them from coming to Me; for the kingdom of heaven belongs to such as these.'" (Matthew 19:14)

> Few things touch my heart as deeply as the voice of a child in fervent prayer.

> J.R. (age seven) said in a quiet car today: "Mom, do you ever just think how AMAZING God is?!" —Yes, like right then!

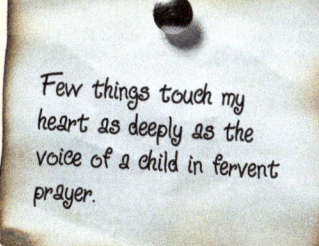

Valentine's Posing Pansies

Happy Valentine's Day!

Dear Lindsey,

Chris and I have never been much for the typical Hallmark holidays. We love each other and tell each other regularly…in our own ways. It might be my making his favorite meal or his taking the kids so I can go for a walk *alone* on a sunny afternoon. We each have love languages that are outside of Chapman's book, but it is good because we have discussed it and both agree our language is right for us. (Shouldn't chocolate be another love language? Or fishing? Or…oops, I am off my story.)

I love that for our anniversary one year (okay, many years), he stopped at a convenience store and bought me my favorite candy on his way home late at night. Somehow, it makes me feel special that he trusts me not to be a high-maintenance girl, and he can count on me to not be needy when he is living life for a purpose, our purpose. I know it's weird, but it flatters me just the same. Of course, I have never been offended by his brag-worthy gifts, either!

For his birthday, I spell "Happy Birthday" with cookies since he likes them better than cake, and I am confident that it is one gift he cannot get for himself. I guess that's how we speak love in the Brady house.

But one Valentine's Day a few years ago, he decided to dare to be different. Or actually, he dared to be typical, since he was usually different. He dared to get me the typical Valentine's gift: a dozen red roses.

I am guessing he planned on walking in and creating a dramatic moment, carrying the lovely vase of abnormally gorgeous flowers in full bloom. He probably imagined his bride descending the stairs and covering him with grateful kisses while kids *ooh*ed and *aah*ed by our side. He knew the "typical" would be a surprise in itself, since it was different than our norm.

But I was not home. He had forgotten it was my day with the homeschool group at church.

By the time I got home, the flowers were proudly displayed on the kitchen island. Immediately putting my nose to them to take in the fragrance, I realized they were silk. Silk? Yes, fake flowers. I tried to think through his reasoning:

> "Silk flowers will prevent her allergies from bothering her."

> "Silk flowers will last forever, while real flowers will die away."

> "Silk flowers look perfect and have more vibrant colors."

> "Terri likes silk, which is why she had them at our wedding." (In reality, we had silk wedding flowers because we got married Mother's Day weekend, and no flower shop would commit to live flowers…oh yeah, and they were cheaper.)

But then I got real:

> "I bet he didn't even notice they were fake. He probably stopped at the store and was on the phone. He grabbed the first thing he saw, paid with a credit card, and brought them home."

When he was done with his conference call, I went into his office and told him thanks for the Valentine's Day flowers. He never explained the silk, and I never mentioned it. He was beaming that I was pleased.

The next day, I couldn't hide it any longer.

"Did you know those flowers were fake?" I asked him in his office, mid-morning.

Pause…

…Long pause…

"Are you kidding?" He looked up at me with those sparkly eyes, which seemed to be restraining the grin to sheepishness. "The flowers are fake?"

I giggled. "Yes."

I continued, in order to relieve his awkwardness and bring the humor we both love, "Let me guess: you stepped into the flower store at 90 miles an hour and picked up the prettiest thing you saw. You couldn't get off the phone, patiently waiting while someone was talking in your ear; you

My thirteen-year-old to his brother: "You have to learn to work hard. And your wife can do all of the thinking."

paid for the order and brought it home to the counter, never noticing that you had purchased silk flowers."

"Guilty as charged," he said, with a full-out grin, which burst to laughter. "I even held it carefully with one hand on the passenger seat, trying not to spill the water on the way home!" He laughed some more.

A man who can laugh at himself is easy to love.

The flowers didn't make me sneeze.

They were vibrant and colorful.

They made a beautiful year-round decoration, and even survived a move or two.

They reminded me that I married the man of my dreams as a playmate. The humor of the situation bonded our marriage further and was truly my favorite Valentine's present ever.

> *Any Prince Charming could have given me flowers. Mine gave me a story.*

May you cherish the stories with your Valentine!

Love,

Terri

Whippoorwill Wakening

Dear Lindsey,

Whippoor…will…

Whippoor…will.

"Yes!" Excitement filled me when I recognized the early bird finishing his nightshift, as morning gilded the sky.

Jet lag was over.

The day before, I had slept until 11:00 a.m., wasting half a day of vacation in this beautiful country. I had felt like a grump all day: bothered by the heat, working at the hottest hours, one step behind my family of noisy kids all day.

The eleven-hour flight to Rome had had its usual challenges with four children along. Sleeping on a plane is generally difficult, but when children fight on both sides to use my legs as pillows, my elbow room vanishes, and I am resigned to a still position, attempting to leave their slumber undisturbed.

The price to be paid is jet lag. Some say jet lag is caused by the six-hour time change; I have come to believe its cause is the forty-hours-awake shift that takes days for a body to reconcile.

No longer! *Now* the trip could begin! I was finally awake early enough to enjoy the cool morning with the cacophony of birds as I had my outdoor quiet time.

Scripture, prayer, and foreign birdsongs began the morning. The North Carolina cardinals were as far away as their song was different. A high-pitched squabble broke out far up in the tree to the right; a rooster crowed in the distance behind me; a songbird joyfully welcomed the morning, while another sang loudly as if trying to use volume to

> In Italy on vacation: "Mom, if I keep eating like this (pizza and pasta) every night, I am going to weigh like eighty pounds by the time we get home!"
> —Nate (age twelve)

make up for his lacking of variety in pitches. Melodies were woven together with a bass from the familiar coo of a dove. The music screamed evidence of their Creator who wrote the score.

As I read amid the surrounding orchestra, a familiar sound emerged from the woods. *"Cuckoo!"* Subconsciously, it took me to my grandmother's kitchen in Talladega, Alabama, where a plastic bird would emerge from the wooden clock on the wall every hour. *"Cuckoo! Cuckoo!"* it sang as if purposefully pulling me to consciousness.

I paused in my reading. *"Cuckoo!"* came from my left this time. What a gift the morning has been! The church bell in the distance gonged seven times.

I recognized the answered prayer: that I would awake early enough to be peaceful before the Brady bunch arose. It has been a secret to sanity for all of motherhood. I used to joke to myself, "I have to rise early enough to beat the children up." (The semantics make me laugh every time.) Many mornings, the wakeup call was, well, alarming as a 5:30 a.m. alarm clock in an attempt to "beat up" a baby who seemed to keep waking earlier each day. But buzzing alarm clock memories made the nudging of a whippoorwill more beautiful in contrast, even though both brought blessings.

Years ago, in a Bible study with girlfriends at college, one of them had shared that her first prayer of the day was: "Thank You, God, for waking me."

I remember my own usual reaction to mornings at the time: "Really? That's all the sleep I get?! Ugh!" But that young lady's prayer changed me. I don't even remember her name, but I have thought of her countless mornings when I have had to shift my thinking to: "Thank You, God, for waking me."

Great is Thy faithfulness. Morning by morning, new mercies I see. Help me, Lord, to take time to recognize Your gifts, even in a whippoorwill.

And thanks for waking me.

Terri

My ten-year-old: "God is beast! He oozes awesomeness!"

Balloon Ride to Rome
(Love at Every Altitude)

Dear Lindsey,

I am just arriving home from Rome, Italy! Ah, the beautiful country and people I miss!

Honestly, it could have been a trip to the basement of our first apartment in Hartland, MI, and it would have been almost as good because I had Chris. No phone to pull him in one direction or children to pull me in the other.

The way it came about was really by accident. Chris was planning to meet in Rome with someone regarding future ventures, when the following conversation occurred between us:

> Him: "I think I am going to need you to go to Rome."
>
> Me: "All right, well, I will start working on a babysitter."
>
> Him: "You would go with me?! That would be awesome! I was dreading the trip, hating the time away from you guys, but if you go, it would be so much better!"
>
> Me: "I thought you said, 'I think I am going to need you to go to Rome.'"
>
> Him: "That's okay. If that's how you heard it, it was meant to be. What I said was 'I think I am going to need to go to Rome.'"

The misunderstanding led to an un-misunderstandable display of emotions: his. He was *so* excited at the thought of me coming along; how could I disappoint?

I know what you are thinking: Who would not want to go to Rome? Why would this be a question?

A little insight into me, and you would see that I am frugal, and Rome is not. I am frugal with time away from my children, and business trips with my husband have many options. I have been to Rome several times in the last few years, and although I love Italy, I am a country girl, and Rome is indeed a city. I could go on listing the hundreds of logistical reasons I might need to stay home: the homeschool that's on pace, the diet and exercise just getting back into a routine, the Good Friday service for which I have been practicing with the choir, the garden to put in, the tasks that always seem behind in my life, the fact that we will be going to Italy as a family in a couple of months anyway, needing to book a trip to see my folks in Colorado, etc.

But there was one reason to go: the excitement that was on my husband's face at the thought of it.

Sometimes, I come upon a woman who feels it is her lifetime job to be the string and weight attached to her husband's balloon, to keep him down to earth where he belongs. Maybe she's not even a string and weight but a wet cloth, lying on top, between the man and his dreams, to make sure no heat gets through. Quite honestly, the thought runs through my head every time, "That could have been me!"

When Chris first came to me, while we were in engineering school, with the thought of racing Baja trucks across the desert, I put down the idea with the biggest balloon tugging I could muster. Not married, or engaged for that matter, we had received a wonderful gift from God: good timing of a deep conversation.

"So you like me if I am a good-little-engineering student who wants a nine-to-five job at a manufacturing company, but you would have issues if I wanted to do something a little off your defined beaten path?" he asked.

"No...." I had to deny the accusation because, of course, I knew that kind of conditional love was wrong, but I really didn't have any other reason for telling him that the Baja race sounded like a waste of time—and dangerous too! Deep down, I was dangerously close to loving the prideful answer I could give when describing the man I was dating: "an engineer." A Baja driver? Not so much.

I look back now and see a young couple beginning to get to know each other. I saw God laying out the stepping-stones of what would be: riding in a balloon in the ups and downs of life, often with his balloon soaring high and me trying to catch him.

The Baja dream was only the beginning of my big dreamer's crazy dreams unfolding. During our engagement, he told me of his desire to be a published author, as he loves to write. I was thrilled that he felt comfortable enough to reveal his real dreams, despite my prior Baja put-downs; I prayed I would not apply the dreaded damp cloth. One year into our marriage, he announced (after hiding it from me for four months!—probably aware of my damp-cloth tendency) that he had heard about a new business venture, and he thought it was his way to get free from a job. I felt my grip of the balloon string loosening because I finally didn't desire to yank it down but watched to see where it would go.

His dreams continued to fuel his balloon, which seemed to have some valuable hot air as it soared to get free from his engineering job (and me from mine, too): write his first eight books, own a second home in Florida, vacation for a month at a time in Italy, and the "crazy dream" list could go on. But by the grace of God, I stopped trying to pull down on the string in those first months when the income from that new business was thirty-six dollars. It was then that I really wasn't sure if God had created him to be a high flyer, but I *did* know that God had not created me to be his ballast weight.

Fast-forward to now and his recent excitement over my going along on the trip to Rome. There was much more to this. It wasn't that he just *didn't* want me pulling down his string but that he *wanted* me to ride alongside. I don't know if my analogy would have us in the basket of a hot-air balloon together or flying balloons side by side, but regardless, I am thrilled to be the one with whom he chooses to fly. Our balloon ride has had lows of collapsed restaurant ownerships and serious illnesses, wrecked cars and bug-infested basement apartments, but I am grateful that we were riding together at all those altitudes. Sometimes the highest-flying days were simple picnics watching a sunset, mountain biking in the neighborhood, or having a paddle ball game in the park as a break from our intense studying.

Girlfriend, if I had any advice for myself of twenty years ago, it would be: Dear Terri, When you've been given a man who wants to fly, encourage him to fly to the highest potential for which God created him; resist any urge to pull him down.

If I had thoughts to share with a sister presently in the midst of demands of motherhood, they would be: Sometimes the damp cloth needs to be applied to the tasks that wait at home (and will still be waiting upon return) because when your husband asks, "Would you ride in the balloon with me?" it's time to climb into the basket and soar. Whether you go to a park, the basement apartment, or Rome, Italy, soaring in a beautiful balloon together just might result in a soaring, beautiful marriage.

God bless,

Terri

Be Still!—for Your Ears' Sake

Dear Lindsey,

"Both my noses are clogged!" My then six-year-old son woke me in the darkness of morning. I consoled the patient and dug for remedies while my mind realized that it was nighttime to him, but this was my early morning. Now, not only was I missing my last couple winks of sleep before my alarm sounded at 5:30, but soon my exercise time and Bible time would vanish…again… while I coddled him, allowing him to get needed sleep leaning on me.

I always feel as if I can't fill the needs of my family until my needs have been met, and yet once again, I started my day of filling their needs while my tank was empty, despite my intentions. The clock continued its never-ending race while I ran laps up and down the stairs to rouse children for their school day.

> "The only way to slow down life is to be in the moment. Be there."
> —Laurie Woodward

Breakfast; breakfast dishes; wipe the counters (after the six-year-old had already wiped them); split up sibling squabbles; clean up dog mess; wipe tears over the "eaten" toy; get to the car to take the oldest to school and then back home quickly to get the other three started in their homeschool around 8:30. This was the daily routine of the Brady school year.

We had our family Bible time, then math, grammar, the regular subjects; I switched from one subject to the next, sometimes teaching one child while spinning plates in the background with two who didn't have my full attention at the time. The day continued at breakneck speed. I looked forward to after school, when all were settled, and I had an hour of silence before heading out with the taxi-full to evening activities.

That's when the eleven-year-old said, "Can you cut my hair before pictures next week?"

"Sure!" I said, as if it were an easy task. The week's schedule flashed through my mind. Weekend travel and weeknight activities, concerts, and the like made me realize that my "hour of silence" that afternoon would once again be taken by something more urgent: haircuts before pictures next week.

Cutting my boys' hair began as a money-saving venture when we had one child. It grew into an ear-saving venture, when my second son wouldn't sit still long enough and I was worried the "ear-ritated" barber would cut off his ear. (Sorry; I couldn't resist the pun!) But at this stage in my life, the currency being saved was time. I could cut three boys' hair in forty-five minutes, which is how long I would have to wait before even starting at some salons.

I began with the oldest and worked my way down to the youngest. I probably should have used the opposite sequence because by the time I got to the six-year-old with a cold, my patience had waned lower than his.

"Be still, please," I said as I went over the top. He squirmed side to side and tilted his head at every snip.

"Be still," I said more firmly, worried I would clip his ear, but hardly slowing my scissors.

> J.R. (age seven) at 8:00 a.m.: "Mom, I burned 1,000 calories on the treadmill this morning; I don't think I've even eaten that much today!"

"Be still!" I practically shouted at him as I continued my race to get it done before the evening schedule commenced.

Psalm 46:10 abruptly came to my mind: "Be still, and know that I am God!"

I smiled to myself, thinking of God shouting to me to "be still!" with an exclamation point, or else He would chop off my ear.

Regret filled me as I realized how "not still" my day was. I felt like promising I would do better tomorrow. "Tomorrow, I will have a quiet time with You." "Tomorrow, I will have a less rushed day of motherhood." "Tomorrow, I will *be still* and know that You are God."

As quickly as I made promises, I wondered what part of my day I was supposed to have done differently.

> *Was I supposed to tell the sick child to "go back to bed! I want to be with Jesus now!"?...I don't think so.*
>
> *Should I have skipped breakfast or lunch so I could "have a quiet time"?!...Not necessarily.*

> Christine (age eight): "J.R., you didn't burn 1,000 calories on the treadmill; you forgot that point thingy in there. It means it's less."

Should I stop homeschooling or take kids out of activities, so I can sit around with my me-time and make it God-time?

What am I doing wrong?!

A. W. Tozer, in his book *Pursuit of God*, hit me hard. I wasn't born when he wrote the book, but his seeds were planted for a harvest in my lifetime and eternity, I'm sure. In chapter ten, he talks about *me!*

> "No, Dad, I don't trust you to cut my hair. You're the type of guy that I'd be bloody and you'd say, 'Suck it up.'"
> —my ten-year-old, smiling

The day of the haircuts was as though I was saying, "Sorry, I have to do all of this menial stuff called life, but God, I want to be with You. And tomorrow morning, while it is still dark, *then* will be my sacred life."

The conflict comes when I try to separate my "sacred" life and my "secular" life.

The "stillness" God wants from me is that my sacred life and my secular life *are one*. It is then that I truly can be still.

I Corinthians 10:31 says that whether we eat or drink, we should do it all for the glory of God. It means a lot to me that it says "eating and drinking"—such "menial stuff called life."

Be still, and recognize the gift of motherhood He gave.

Be still, and be thankful for the usefulness of my life; I have something to exhaust me every day!

Be still, and praise God!…while I go to work, attend school, cut hair, drive the car pool, and coddle the sick one.

> "Be still—because God is not."
> —Stephen Davey

But don't wait for quiet time to do it. Believe me: I *love* quiet time, and set my alarm clock early on purpose. But if God's purpose for me wakes me before the clock, I can't second-guess His plans for my day. It is then that I can be still and know that He had it planned just perfectly all along.

I suppose being still has little to do with cutting off ears and more to do with opening them to hear God's plan for the day.

May you enjoy this day the Lord planned for you!

Love,

Terri

Always?

Dear Lindsey,

"He's pulling my shirt!" the four-year-old cried while I pried his twenty-two-month-old brother from his shirt on the airplane. We were snuggled—three people into two seats—so the "baby" could ride for free on my lap. It seemed like such a good idea when we qualified for an all-expenses-paid trip to Hawaii. All expenses were paid for Chris and me, so frequent flyer miles paid for one son, and the other was left as a "lap child."

The ten-hour flight from Detroit to Honolulu was better than other connections, and we could take just one more skip over the pond to the island of Kona. The palm trees, the mango juice, the pineapple boat ice cream sundae, the mama whales and baby whales, the seventy-degree-nights and eighty-degree-days were there for us! And coffee. Yes, Kona coffee! Anyone could have predicted it would be challenging to take a long flight with two young boys, but what flight struggle could compare to the islands that awaited our arrival?

I had prepared: Color Wonders would keep the ink off the airplane tray. (Airlines must be thankful for Crayola's invention!) Pre-electronic reader days, I brought books to read aloud, balancing the weight of my carry-on bag with the entertainment provided. A puzzle car-track would fit just right on the airplane tray, and I could imagine whiling away at least a couple of hours as we watched the wind-up car go in circles on our designed track. And then we would redesign the puzzle pieces to make a new track over and over. Hours of happily entertained children translated to a nap or book for me. Cheerios, raisins, granola bars, and canned chicken (for my son with food allergies) would provide the snack time, as well as string out the eating to take longer; that way, more of the ten-hour flight would certainly vanish.

> Christine (age eight) at Red Lobster: "Mom, the milk is only 1 percent milk on the kids' menu. Crazy! What's the other 99 percent?"

I had bought a new running suit for the trip. It was the kind that was too cute to ever bear sweat but perfectly comfortable for a long ride. It was like public-approved pajamas. Matching, unstained clothes for the boys would make cute photos as Hawaiians adorned us with leis upon arrival. I couldn't wait!

Now, as I sat on the plane, I couldn't believe how the infamous Murphy and his laws had decided to join us for this trip!

- The plane was delayed five hours in the terminal, using up most of my entertainment stash.

- We boarded and sat for an additional two hours before taking off for our ten-hour flight; I really don't remember why because I was trying to be Super Mom.

- We never found food without allergens in the airport, so my son had eaten all the canned chicken before the airplane meal arrived.

- The Cheerios spilled all over the floor of the airplane within thirty minutes (*before* takeoff); I kept daydreaming of how to design a Dustbuster for a diaper bag.

- The wind-up car for the track got over-wound within its first run and was never able to be used (despite that, I had to carry the track puzzle pieces to Hawaii and back).

- We accidentally left the spill-proof sippy cups in the airport. (Of course, they are never really spill-proof. Anyway, I always needed them to be "losing-proof." Maybe I needed to attach sippy cups to their hands like the mittens that are strung through their coats.)

- Without a sippy cup, the twenty-two-month-old spilled the apple juice the flight attendant gave him in a Styrofoam cup…all over my new running suit.

- After the food ran out, the allergy-boy lived on potato chips and juice—but no worries: there were only seven hours left in the flight. Certainly, he would sleep for some of those after such an exciting day!

- The diapers ran out in the eighth hour, and the flight attendant graciously provided me with some—four sizes too small.

- What comes after lack of sleep, topped with a diet of potato chips and juice? Diarrhea. When an almost-two-year-old wore a diaper for a six-month-old, it meant my new jogging suit had a new stench, besides the original juice bath.

- Now the brothers were exhausted to the point that shirt-pulling was a tear-jerking, judge-summoning offense.

We were exhausted when the words finally came across the loudspeaker, "Ladies and gentlemen, please prepare for arrival."

As I started to reach down to gather our things, I realized that *now* both boys were asleep…for the last twenty minutes of the seventeen-hour trip. Ugh.

We landed, and as we disembarked, the beautiful Hawaiian girls in hula skirts put flower leis around each of our necks—as if something between my clothing and my nose could disguise the odor.

But Murphy had not left us yet.

We joined the line of weary travelers waiting to see about connections. As we approached the desk, the airline employee's face lit up, and she explained that we had missed our 9:00 p.m. connection, but another one had been delayed and was probably still "over there" (in the other terminal), but we would have to run.

We bolted as fast as possible. Carrying bags of broken toys and lugging drained children who sniffled in exhaustion, Chris and I ran through the doors to the other terminal to the exact gate where the flight was.

Or was not. Not only was the flight gone, but so were the people. The terminal had exactly four people in it: us. The lights were dimmed as if we had somehow snuck into a closed terminal. Disgusted, we turned to walk or stomp back to the original long line of weary people. When we got to the first terminal, we discovered it was now locked. Since no more planes were leaving, I guess they decided to lock the entrance, and we were outside. We waited several minutes until someone inside noticed and let us back in—to go back to the gate and stand at the *end* of the line of weary travelers, so we could book a hotel and flights for the following day.

I tried to forget that my parents from Colorado would already be in Kona waiting for us, since we had invited them to multiply the fun. I tried to forget all our friends who had also qualified for the trip and were probably already in their soft beds with the Hawaiian breeze gently blowing across their bellies full of mango juice. I tried not to calculate that this would mean our trip was one-sixth shorter because of these delays.

I was beginning to stew. I had held it in *all day*. I had tried to be positive for the kids, forgiving to the airline (they knew not what they had done). But **this lady, this airline employee** who had made us **run** all the way to the other terminal **had to have known** what she was doing. **She must have thought it was a funny joke. She was going to pay!**

> Tonight a neighbor boy (age six) stopped by to see if my son could play, but we were eating dinner. "Okay, I'll come back in six minutes," he said.

The "bad wolf" in my head recited the riot act I would be giving the lady as soon as it was my turn at the counter. The "good wolf" on my other shoulder tried to counter, but it was no use: the "bad wolf" was too strong.

The baby whined in tears in the stroller; my silent voices alternated between whining and ranting inside my head.

While I stood in line, my older son started walking in circles around my legs. He held his hands on my knees, as if going around a Maypole, singing a happy song as he walked.

> "If my life is fruitless, it doesn't matter who praises me, and if my life is fruitful, it doesn't matter who criticizes me."
> —John Bunyan

I was so annoyed that even my precious child's voice was on my nerves, and I was just about to ask him to be quiet when I stopped and heard what song he was singing:

"Rejoice in the Lord always; again I say, rejoice! Rejoice in the Lord always; again I say, rejoice! Rejoice! Rejoice! Again I say, rejoice! Rejoice! Rejoice! Again I say, rejoice!"[48]

I couldn't help but think that God had used my son to relay a message that day: Rejoice! Not sometimes. Not when I feel like it. Not when someone else deserves it. But always. Again I say, rejoice!

I can only imagine the airline employees' lives I was about to lambaste with negativity when the Lord interrupted with my son's song.

So I had only five wonderful days in Hawaii instead of six; was it really that big a deal?

In the end, Murphy loses; God wins. I am on the winning team, and I need to act like it. Always!

> "Rejoice in the Lord always; again I say, rejoice!" (See Philippians 4:4.)

Love ya!

Terri

> An adorable two-year-old in the hotel elevator this past weekend said, "I love riding in refrigerators!"

And to My Listening Ear

Dear Lindsey,

What a week! We have enjoyed some time at our lake home. I hesitate to call it "vacation," since we are still actively online, with phones and extra travel, but we are vacationing from the scheduled soccer and school. God's artistry in sunrises, sunsets, and everything else seems so beautiful when reflected on water.

Reflections on Water Can Lead to Reflections on Life.

I love early morning fishing with my kids. I select one (or sometimes two) of my children, put them in a canoe with a trolling motor and some poles and lures, and we head out to watch the sunrise while we entice the unseen creatures below.

Why Early?

At 5:30 a.m., the lake is serene: no boat wakes or phones to contend with, no schedules to compete for my kids' time, just peace outside of their voices and mine. Oh yeah, and some say the fish bite more at dawn.

Why Photos?

The entire family doesn't fit into our three-seated vessel, so we share our victories via camera. Sometimes, on a day without bites, it is fun to go through the photos, to remember the big ones will come!

But It's Not about the Fish

"Mom, it doesn't matter if we catch any fish today," my eight-year-old serenely said as the trolling motor left a silent *V* sketched in the placid lake behind us. "It is just nice being with you."

It is a time of reflection—of the new sun off the mirror of water and of my kids' thoughts of this turning world. They ask questions in those peaceful hours that maybe get lost in our ninety-miles-per-hour days.

"Do you think I am not catching fish today because I sin too much?"

>Pensive.

"Is it ever okay to get angry because…didn't Jesus get angry?"

>Fighting strong, but wanting answers with a friend along at 5:45 a.m.!

My kids' discussion questions roll out with the line behind the boat. I just want to make sure they know that I am here; I have a listening ear; I am ready with open arms when the storms send unsettling waves. If they don't know that when they're eight, they won't know to look for it when they're eighteen.

I *love* our early times together. I couldn't help but see the parallel to morning quiet times with God.

Quiet Time with God

Why Early?

Before the sun, the world is serene: no waves or phones to contend with, no schedules to compete with the time, except for the pillow—the evil opponent!

Why a Notebook?

Like a photo to share with family, a notebook records my wrestling moments, my tearful prayer requests, and the gut-wrenching thoughts that once prevented my sleep. The answers received

---

"Mom, when can we discuss the next lesson in *Pursuit of Holiness* (by J. Bridges)?" —my fourteen-year-old during family vacation

through these early morning times with Him are revealed when I read the journal years later. It encourages me: today's resolution will come in His timing, too.

But it's not about the ritual; it's about the relationship.

It is a time when I can tell Him, "It's okay if I don't catch anything today; I just enjoy being with You."

In His Word, I am reminded that He is here. He has a listening ear; He is ready with open arms when the storms send unsettling waves—which sometimes are the lure that got me there in the first place.

"Don't let your child be the 'one that got away'" is the advertisement line from Zebco fishing equipment. Maybe someone at that company had some good fishing conversations with his kids too.

Girlfriend, don't be the one who got away from God. As Rick Warren says:

"If you feel far from God right now, guess who moved."[49]

Tomorrow: Tell the pillow to have a good day without you. Grab a pen, a notebook, and a Bible, and enjoy a relationship with Him. Read, pray, speak, and listen.

> "Failure in my life almost always begins with a famine of God's Word and prayer."[50]
> —Anne Graham Lotz

> "It's better to be sleep deprived than God deprived."[51] —Jill Briscoe

Eternally His,

Terri

Nate (age eleven): "Mom, when I'm having trouble forgiving someone, I just think of Joseph. He forgave his brothers after they sold him as a slave!"

During this morning's Bible time, we read Luke 2:16, "and found Mary and Joseph and the babe lying in a manger." My five-year-old said, "All three?!"

Shine on a Parade

Dear Lindsey,

My mom woke me one Pennsylvania morning on my birthday and told me God had wrapped my present in white, if I would just look outside. *(Snow!)* Although I had always wished for one of those cool pool-party birthdays my friends had in the summer, my parents had a way of making my birthday special just five days before Christmas.

Mom never wrapped my birthday present in Christmas paper but went through the inconvenience of getting the "out of season" birthday paper to make my day different. I was the envy of my brothers (I was sure) when I got presents two days in the same week.

Then some adult came and rained on my parade.

"You must hate having a Christmas birthday!" the adult said.

What's there to hate? was my thought, but what I said at that young age was "Yeah," in agreement with the adult, and my heart searched for reasons to hate it.

I am reminded of this every June 10 because I remember a time someone rained on my son's parade. That date was already special to me because it is my friend's birthday, but then we became parents on June 10, an answer to many prayers! The value of June 10 multiplied when our second son was *also* born on that same date three years later.

I have painted their shared birthday with a positive brush, the same way my mother had painted my Christmas birthday. My boys always get double cakes. (Although sometimes they help me, and one requests cupcakes, cookies, or cookie dough instead!) Their uncles often call one, hang up, and then call the other so they get double calls. They can party together—and will have it in common all through adulthood. *And* they can sing the song, "You say it's your birthday? It's my birthday too, yeah!" and really mean it!

Casey was four or five when some adult came into his life and said, "You must hate sharing a birthday with your brother. That stinks." I watched my son's sky turn a little gray as he probably contemplated why it was a bad thing; he had never known any different.

It must be easier to rain on a parade than to shine on one.

When my milk-allergic son was two, eating a frozen banana covered with sprinkles, enjoying every minute of it, someone at the store decided to shower some rain: "You can never have ice cream? Never? I couldn't *live* if I were you!"

Someone recently drizzled on my daughter, "You might be able to put dew from the grass on your face and wipe off those freckles."

I know, I know: some of those negative comments are from people just trying to be fun. Some are trying to relate, but too often, un-contemplated words are just a form of precipitation on a parade! (My husband has spent hours counting the freckles on my daughter's face, so I am thinking the "wiping the freckles off" comment didn't stick, but I could practically see her thoughts: "Am I *supposed* to want to wipe them off?")

Small talking at graduation parties recently, I saw my own tendency toward rain as thoughts crossed my mind during conversations. It *is* easier to bring up negative subjects, spread negative news, or, in other words, rain on the parade. But we are not called to the easier path. We *can* paint some positive into peoples' lives. What if we encouraged the mother of the handicapped child, instead of pointing out how difficult her life is? (She already knew that part.) What if we told the person getting married that he is going to *love* married life, instead of pointing out the ball and chain? What if we stop negatively saying, "You sure have your hands full!" to the mom with five young kids in the store and instead say, "Wow, I bet you have some joyful times coming in your house!" What if we told someone in a storm of life that without the rain, a sun can never make a rainbow?

Do you remember someone who brought out the sun in your parade called life?

I remember "messing up" (I thought) a reading at church during the Christmas program when I was ten. Afterward, the minister's wife came to me, as if she hadn't even heard my error, and said, "You are a beautiful reader!"

Her husband immediately interjected, "And you read well too!"

Ha! That one pierced through some clouds.

Once as a teen, when I had burned cookies and my brothers were making fun as brothers do, my father came in, took a bite, and exclaimed, "Finally! Cookies made just the way I like them!" That one still makes me smile—shining sun onto my parade thirty years later!

A most memorable sun shone into my life in February 2010. A man sent an e-mail to my husband with the subject title, "Should there be a second author in the Brady house?" This was a strange, out-of-the-blue comment from someone I was yet to meet. Attached to the letter was a fifteen-page pdf presentation encouraging me to write. Apparently Russ Mack, who had helped get Chris's bestseller published, had seen me speak on stage somewhere with Chris. The first page of his document had a copy of the "*New York Times* Bestselling Author" award from my husband's book *Launching a Leadership Revolution*, but Russ had Photoshopped an *s* on the end, so the ribbon now said, "*New York Times* Bestselling Authors."

For fifteen pages, Russ quoted Benjamin Franklin ("We should all write something worth reading or live something worth writing") and others and told me "Somewhere, somebody is looking for exactly what you have to offer." Since he was involved in marketing books, there was weight to his opinion that was both flattering and humbling to me. His sun was high in the sky, shining on my parade.

Despite little response from me and nothing in it for him, his encouragement didn't stop. A few weeks later, he e-mailed me again to see if I had thought through his proposal. I must admit, I couldn't figure out why he would continue encouraging me, especially since I had told him, "Thanks, but no, thanks."

In 2011, another letter came: "It looks like the world still needs your wisdom." Later that year, within one week of the first letter of my blog, LetterstoLindsey.com, Russ sent me *another* e-mail telling me he knew it would be a success. I was shocked he had already found my blog, since I had not told him. Another letter came the next year. His sun shone brightly and consistently.

Although I only actually met him once or twice, I consider Russ's encouragement a true blessing. *He was a real sun on my parade.*

But suns set.

Last week, Russ's sun set, when he lost his battle to cancer and went to be with the Lord.

Though I did not know him well, I can tell you that the effects of his sun will warm and give light to my life and the lives of many others.

> May we each follow his example of shining onto the parades of others' lives.
>
> Encourage when there's nothing in it for you.
>
> Encourage again, even if there's no acknowledgment.
>
> Be positive toward others, even when you feel like your life is a little cloudy, and you will be surprised how the sun reflects back on your own parade.
>
> And one day, like Russ, when your sun has set, the effects will shine on the parades of others for years to come.

Go bless,

Terri

"Therefore encourage one another and build each other up, just as in fact you are doing." (1 Thessalonians 5:11, NIV)

Sticky note: My son (age six) just comforted my daughter (age eight) after a skinned knee: "You can have my Band-Aid off of my thumb. Here." Awww!

Sunrise, Sunset—Fishing for Memories

Dear Lindsey,

There have been many times when I have felt like I was not thriving but barely surviving motherhood. By far, one of the most challenging was when my youngest was crying all the time. Funny, but as is often the case with twenty/twenty hindsight, I can see a tremendous blessing that came from that desperate time: something that came to be called "early morning fishing."

Although the crying baby took so much attention, his sister, only nineteen months his senior, was not exactly changing her own diapers either. I can remember her recognizing the opportunity for mischief when I was nursing the baby. She would wait until I was occupied with him; then she would run to get the wipes and pull them out one by one, putting them on her head or wiping my mirrors or going for something just out of reach, but not dangerous enough for me to stop what I was doing—just more mess. The days would go by, and I would feel as though my punch-in clock had actually reversed. There was more on my to-do list and nothing crossed off. All I did was clean up messes that weren't even there when the day had begun. No progress. Had I even seen "the boys" that day?

For the five years before boy number three arrived, we had referred to our first two children as "the boys," and then we had the baby girl. "You bring 'the boys,' and I will bring the baby," was how we spoke. Now that there was another boy, it seemed odd if not impossible to break our habit, so we continued referring to the older ones as "the boys" and the next two as "the little ones," which were the exact terms my parents had used for my brothers and me, coincidentally.

I was convinced that in and among the crying baby and needy toddler, "the boys" were being neglected. In two years, their world had been turned upside down with lack of Mommy time, not to mention that we were building a new home at the same time.

My solution: take them "early morning fishing."

I am sure that to many, this seems like a perfect job for Dad, but my husband prefers sleeping at sunrise (since he reads late into the night) and is not much for fishing any time of day, so it was the perfect opportunity for me to educate the boys and spend quality time away from crying babies.

Since we could not trust getting a cell phone signal, I would take one walkie-talkie and leave the other one with Chris, next to the bed, so he could get in touch with me when the crier awoke. The boys and I would head to the lake in the backyard, using a Polaris Ranger to navigate the hill. My goal was to get there, get the canoe out of the barn and the trolling motor attached, and be afloat before the sky was lit. This gave us about one hour, plus or minus. Even during the school year, we could be out on the lake and back by 7:45 a.m., ready to attack the day. The boys had to be able to tie their own line and take a fish off the hook in order to participate in the privilege of early morning fishing. It was never hard to wake them when fish were waiting.

What memories we have! From my walking on water when I realized there was a snake in the boat with us, to feeding the nest of spiders to the fish, to singing "Great Is Thy Faithfulness" as the sun crested the trees, to the treble-hook in my cheek from my son's casting error, to the thirty-nine-inch pike, the big ones that got away, and the kids that didn't; God blessed us with some wonderful mornings.

When in Florida on vacation last week, I was thrilled to accept my now-fourteen-year-old's invitation to go early morning fishing. "Thank you for teaching us to tie lines and take fish off when we were little," my eleven-year-old told me. "It's so easy now." The one who was the "crying baby" is six, and the tears are forgotten, as he too has earned his spot in the boat. (Of course, we needed the bigger boat.)

I took photos last week and paused to take in the moment. That tall, handsome, drawn-out body of my teenager's silhouette in the gorgeous dawning light made my heart flash back to the little boy who started the tradition, with the big orange life jacket hindering his every move.

As the song says, "Sunrise, sunset. Swiftly fly the years."[52] I guess I can really thank God for my crying baby because in my desperation, it led to a blessing of memories and traditions that outlasted the tears.

Thanks be to Him,

Terri

> From the backseat of the car on the way to Pennsylvania today: "Cows smell like number two because they don't wipe."
> —J.R. (age six)

> J.R. (age six) said, "I know who is US President; I just don't know who is Advice President."

> My son (age six) just saw the crack in my windshield. He said, "Wow! That fly must have hit hard!" Hahaha!

> "And they were sore afraid (from Luke 2)" was quoted today by J.R. (age six) as "and they were sorta afraid."

ized*

The Ring

Dear Lindsey,

My mother handed me the ring with a deep grin that punctuated the significance of the gift. It was a tiny ring, just right for my seven-year-old finger. "This is a *real* diamond," she said, handing me the tiny fraction of a karat in a size 4 band. She explained that she had bought the ring before I was born and saved it for when I was old enough to wear it. I could hardly believe she would allow me to hold it—much less have it in *my* size! I thanked her and felt that special warmth in my heart my tomboyish buffalo skin normally tried to repel. I headed out to play.

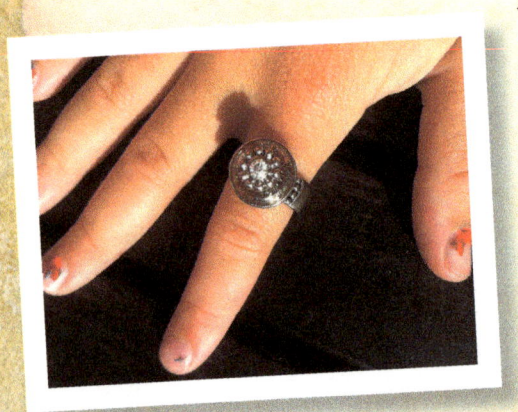

Tetherball was a favorite sport of mine. The two-person game involved standing on either side of a pole that had one ball tethered to it from the top. One would hit the ball clockwise, while his opponent tried to hit it counterclockwise with greater force. As the opponents smacked the ball, it gained potential for more height. My trick was to hit it with strength at the angle to send it just out of my opponent's reach, elliptically landing back within my reach so I could send it in the same pattern again the next time around. The game increased speed as the tether shortened, wrapping around the pole, until the tether was tightened to the last inch, proclaiming the winner.

It was at the end of such a game in the neighbors' backyard when I realized that the ring I had possessed for less than twenty-four hours was gone. I searched below the pole, combing the grass with my fingers to no avail.

Heart-broken, and mad at myself, I couldn't help but think that maybe I should have been "a good little girl" playing with dolls or makeup like other girls instead—then I would not have lost

200

the ring. I sinfully didn't tell my mother about the loss because I figured it would take her a few weeks to notice, and that would sound better than, "I lost it in the first twenty-four hours."

"Besides," I thought, *"I didn't want that ring anyway. Who wants something that doesn't even stay on during tetherball?!"*

It was my nature: When I felt defeated, I would convince myself that whatever I didn't get (or couldn't keep) was something I didn't want anyway. It was easier than admitting I needed to change.

Anniversary Gift

On our tenth wedding anniversary, Chris decided to get me a ring. The buffalo in me liked the idea of a simple anniversary band, with no "annoying stones" to get snagged on my pockets when they warmed my hands. Chris had a different idea.

The solitaire was a diamond to be admired by any passerby. The round cut magnified the colors that only God could place in such a gorgeous gem. Its clarity drew in light, seemingly multiplying it in the reflection with a disco-ball effect on the ceiling of the store, to my embarrassment. "We'll take it!" Chris said, while I shied away, telling him, "No way!" But inside, I felt pretty just being treated as pretty.

The store sized it to fit my finger like a glove, although any glove worth working would not fit on this ring without getting caught. Chris glowed with pride as we traveled to the resort where we were staying that night. We had a beautiful evening celebrating our first decade together, and I wore my ring with pride, almost wanting to point it out to strangers, as I did my engagement ring the night he popped the question in Pittsburgh, PA a decade prior.

I felt loved.

The next morning, I rose early and headed outside to enjoy the sunrise for my quiet time with God. As I recorded the previous evening's shopping and date in the journal of my mind, a feeling of sadness surrounded me. I felt like a phony. *"I don't even LIKE rings. I forget to put on jewelry that I already have! I am not pretty*

> "Your value doesn't decrease based on someone's inability to see your worth."
> —Amy Marks

enough to have people looking at my hands. My nails are chipped; my hands are rough because I don't know how to 'act like a lady.' I cannot fake this. I am not the jewelry-kind-of-girl. Did he forget who I am? Where I have been? I am not worthy of its cost, much less its beauty!"

As I continued trying to read my Bible, the self-degrading thoughts continued. I started planning how to return the ring and how I would tell Chris. Tears trickled down my cheeks, thinking about how we would owe the store for the custom sizing, even if they gave us our money back. Regret overcame me as I realized I had worn it the night before as a phony—mesmerized by its sparkle, as if that fit me. The conflict was still vibrant in my heart when Chris awoke and came outside to where I was sitting.

> The enemy is winning if our mind is occupied more with guilt than with our gifts.

"Are you wearing the ring?!" he excitedly asked as he approached, looking for my hand.

I wiped my eyes and confessed my thoughts to him. "I cannot own a ring like this. I am not meant to wear something so valuable. We need to get it back to the store—today. We can see if they will give us all our money back, even if we have to pay for the sizing. I'm sorry. I have never had such a tremendous case of buyer's remorse."

He stared at me dumbfounded for a split second and then kneeled down on one knee, cupped my face in his hands, and said firmly, "We will not take the ring back. You cannot have buyer's remorse because you did not buy the ring; I did. It is my gift to you. *Now stop insulting me.*"

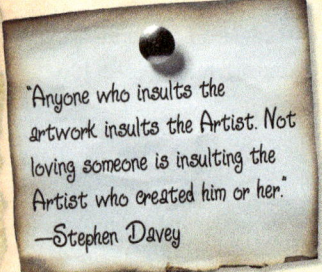

> "Anyone who insults the artwork insults the Artist. Not loving someone is insulting the Artist who created him or her."
> —Stephen Davey

He kissed me as if it were the first time our lips had met.

The tears disappeared from my face. My quickened heart rate sent a cleansing blood through my body. A peace came over me as I realized he loved me so deeply to look beyond what I saw in myself. He didn't give me the ring because of who I was, but because of who he is.

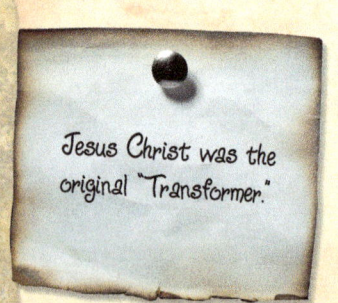

Hating Myself

> Jesus Christ was the original "Transformer."

As I recall that story, another story comes to mind: the one where I say, "I hate myself! Why can't I be like others? I keep doing wrong. I can't change. I will never get better. I am worthless!"

And God gently answers, "I created you. Stop insulting Me. I knitted you to be an original. Your hands are My design. I know the depth of your heart, the chasm of your sins, and I sent my Son, Jesus Christ, to take it all. I have a purpose for every strength you have and for every failure it took to gain that strength. I have a purpose for *EVERY* weakness you possess, since My strength is made perfect in your weakness. You can't change, but I can change you. My purposes are greater than your vision. I created you just the way I intended. I bought you for the price of my Son, and I have no remorse. Now stop insulting Me."

The Gift of Forever

Girlfriend, that eternal salvation is a gift that was bought before you were born to fit you precisely. It is ironic that we cannot have the peace of His gift pumping into our veins until we have the remorse over our sins cleansing the path. No one can comb through the grass to find His gift, and none of us deserves its worth. It is ours because of Who He is, not who we are. He loves us so deeply to look beyond what we see in ourselves. It is amazing that just when we say, "I have such remorse!" He answers, "You can't; I'm the One Who bought you!"

I hope you feel loved – because you are.

I guess I am not a buffalo or a butterfly or even a buffafly after all. I am a new creature in Christ, and I want His glory to reflect from my life like a disco ball!

In Christ,

Terri

"God knitted you before you were born." (Psalm 139:13)

"His strength is made perfect in my weakness." (2 Corinthians 12:9)

"I am a new creature in Christ." (2 Corinthians 5:17)

"Salvation is a gift from God, because of who He is, not who we are." (Ephesians 2:8-9)

"Confess your sins (with remorse) and you will be forgiven." (1 John 1:9)

"The gift of forever: For God so loved the world, that He gave His only begotten Son, that whoever believes in Him shall not perish but have eternal life." (John 3:16)

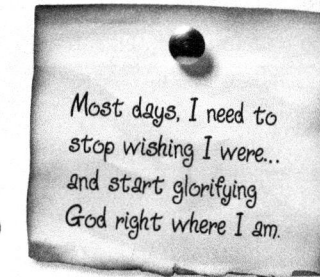

Most days, I need to stop wishing I were... and start glorifying God right where I am.

Acknowledgments

Thank you to the girl in seventh grade who told me I carried my purse wrong—a skill I never knew I needed to acquire. For her and many other critics, I am thankful because I know Christ had a purpose for each one of them and the person I would become in learning to love them.

Thank you to the leadership and members of the churches I have attended. The members of the body of Christ sharpen each other, as iron sharpens iron, and I would not have stories to tell in the light in which they are told without the massive impact of the body of Christ on my life. I wish all people understood that church attendance is not simply for self-satisfaction; each member of the body greatly impacts the others.

To my girlfriends: buffaloes, butterflies, and buffaflies alike, I am forever grateful that God placed you in my life. Whether it is a text you have sent, a comment on the blog, or an e-mail, tweet, or Facebook message, you have impacted me each incident at a time! "Two people are better off than one, for they can help each other succeed. If one person falls, the other can reach out and help. But someone who falls alone is in real trouble" (Ecc 4:9-10, NLT). Oh how I have fallen! You have lifted me higher than I would have thought to lift myself. Laurie Woodward, I am thankful to live this LIFE with you! Jill Guzzardo, Lisa Hawkins, Raylene MacNamara, Debbie Spolar, Sandra Montenegro, and Danae Mattis: You have been vessels of blessings to my life! Tracey Avereyn, Susie Hallstrand, and Jen Korte: I am thankful for the Guatemalan bonding of our souls as sisters in Christ. Anna Huber, no one has taught me more about how to serve one another as if serving the Lord Jesus himself. Rita Haas, Lisa Fotu, Jenny Salter, Marcia Robinson, Pat Tefel, and Kenyon Robson: Your friendship is like an underlying current of happiness for me. Mary Radosa, and Cassie Birtles and of course Lindsey Spiewak: Your humility in encouraging me to write a blog in the stadium's hallway that day made more of a difference than you can know.

To Lalanne Barber: I don't *no wear* I *wood bee* without *you're reeding* my blog. Thank you for often saving us all from reading my original *pour* choice of words—blech!

To the countless people who cooked for me, sewed for me, drove for me, or voluntarily nursed me back to health for months after brain surgery: greater love has no one known.

Letters to Lindsey

To Rob Hallstrand, Deborah Brady (chief editor), Paul Hawley (editor), Wendy Branson (editor), Norm Williams (graphic art and cover design), Dirk Rozich (blog header design), Bill Rousseau (project manager), Jordan Woodward (2nd edition) and Steve Kendall (2nd edition), and the rest of the team on the project: You are amazing! I have no idea how you do what you do, but I am just grateful that you do it! Lives are changed because of you.

To Russ Mack: May you rest in peace, knowing that your words of encouragement for me to write a book were not in vain.

To my in-laws, Jim and Gayle Brady: You are such a blessing in my life!

To my parents, Ron and Sue Estes: Thank you for your unconditional love. I still strive to please you.

To my three brothers, Larry, Tim, and Mike Estes: Thank you for making me feel loved and protected in the way only brothers can. And thanks for forcing me to laugh instead of cry so you wouldn't get into trouble when you jumped off the see-saw at Grandma's, making me fall flat on my belly, and knocking the wind out of me clear to my soul. (Okay, *now* I hope Mom and Dad just read that.) You made me able to smile through a lot.

To my children, Casey, Nate, Christine, and J.R.: Thank you for giving me freedom to tell the stories of our lives together. Your openness in allowing me to share will, Lord willing, help others grow closer as families and grow closer to Christ as well. Your teamwork in our house is what enables Dad and me to do what we do. I pray the seeds that are planted grow into many blessings to you and your future families.

To Chris: No one deserves more acknowledgements for this book coming to fruition. Thank you for believing in me much more than I believe in myself on a daily basis. Thank you for "forcing" me to write a blog. Your influence in the lives of others is so admirable, but your influence in my life is completely immeasurable. Where I say, "Ready, aim…aim…aim…aim…," you yell, "Fire!" in God's perfect timing. Nothing could be more exemplary of that than your publishing this book "behind my back."

To Jesus Christ: You are my all in all. I love you with all my heart and pray You use this book for Your ultimate glory.

In Him,
Terri Brady

Notes

1. Elizabeth Prentiss, *Stepping Heavenward: One Woman's Journey to Godliness* (Uhrichsville, OH: Barbour Publishing Inc., 1998), originally published in 1869.
2. John Gray, Ph.D., *Men Are from Mars, Women Are from Venus* (New York: HarperCollins Publishers, 1992).
3. Dr. Gary Smalley, *For Better or for Best: A Valuable Guide to Knowing, Understanding, and Loving Your Husband* (Grand Rapids, MI: Zondervan, 2012), 29.
4. Bill and Pam Farrel, *Men Are Like Waffles; Women Are Like Spaghetti: Understanding and Delighting in Your Differences* (Eugene, OR: Harvest House Publishers, 2001).
5. Stephen Davey, "Set Apart," *Wisdom for the Heart*, copyright 2013 OnePlace.com, http://www.oneplace.com/ministries/wisdom-for-the-heart/read/articles/set-apart-12255.html.
6. Nicole Johnson's *Dropping Your Rock* (Published by Thomas Nelson October 17, 2011), originally publish in 2003.
7. Amy Grant, "Angels," *Straight Ahead*, Myrrh label, produced by Brown Bannister, released in 1984, album.
8. Urban Dictionary, *fashionista* definition, copyright 1999-2013, www.urbandictionary.com/define.php?term=fashionista.
9. Josh McDowell, live talk at Colonial Baptist Church in August, 2012.
10. Emily Perl Kingsley, "Welcome to Holland," copyright 1987, reprinted in *Dear Abby, Chicken Soup for the Mother's Soul*, etc
11. John Watson (Ian MacLaren), Quote Investigator, June 29, 2010, http://quoteinvestigator.com/2010/06/29/be-kind/.
12. C.S. Lewis, *The Four Loves: The Much Beloved Exploration of the Nature of Love* (New York: Harcourt, Brace, 1960).
13. Gene Edwards, *Exquisite Agony (Crucified by Christians)* (Jacksonville, FL: The SeedSowers, 1994).
14. Oliver DeMille and Orrin Woodward, *LeaderShift: A Call for Americans to Finally Stand Up and Lead* (New York: Business Plus, Hachette Book Group, 2013).
15. Dr. James C. Dobson, *Parenting Isn't for Cowards* (Carol Stream, IL: Tyndale House Publishers Inc., 2007).
16. Dennis and Barbara Rainey, *Passport to Purity Book and CD Pack* (Little Rock: FamilyLife, 2006).
17. Abraham Lincoln, *American Federalist Journal: Foundation Principles for the 21st Century*, copyright 2001-2013, www.federalistjournal.com/ref/quotes1.php.
18. Oliver DeMille, *Thomas Jefferson Education: Teaching a Generation of Leaders for the Twenty-First Century* (Cedar City, UT: George Wythe College Press, 2006.)
19. Oliver DeMille and Orrin Woodward, *LeaderShift: A Call for Americans to Finally Stand Up and Lead* (New York: Business Plus, Hachette Book Group, 2013).
20. Debra Bell, *The Ultimate Guide to Homeschooling* (Anderson, IN: ApologiaPress, 2009).
21. Laurie Parsons and Jeffrey Freed, M.A.T., *Right-Brained Children in a Left-Brained World: Unlocking the Potential of Your ADD Child* (New York: Simon & Schuster, 1997).
22. Robert T. Kiyosaki, *Cashflow Quadrant: Rich Dad's Guide to Financial Freedom* (New York: Warner Books Inc., 2000).
23. Catherine Maurice, *Let Me Hear Your Voice: A Family's Triumph over Autism* (New York: Fawcett Books, 1993).
24. Christine M. Field, *Help for the Harried Homeschooler: A Practical Guide to Balancing Your Child's Education with the Rest of Your Life* (Colorado Springs: WaterBrook Press, 2002).
25. Scott Turansky, D. Min., and Joanne Miller, R.N., B.S.N., *Say Goodbye to Whining, Complaining, and Bad Attitudes…in You and Your Kids!* (Colorado Springs: WaterBrook Press, 2000).
26. Bobby Braddock, "I Wanna Talk about Me," *Pull My Chain*, Dreamworks label, recorded by Toby Keith, produced by James Stroud, released August 20, 2001, compact disc.
27. Dennis and Barbara Rainey, *Building Your Mate's Self-Esteem* (Nashville: Thomas Nelson Inc., 1995).
28. C.J. Mahaney, *Humility: True Greatness* (Sisters, OR: Multnomah Publishers Inc., 2005).
29. C.S. Lewis, @CSLewisDaily, Twitter, copyright 2013, https://twitter.com/CSLewisDaily/status/296446636186558466/photo/1, Jan. 29, 2013.
30. Mike Rutherford and B.A. Robertson, "The Living Years," *Living Years*, Atlantic WEA label, recorded by Mike + The Mechanics, produced by Christopher Neil and Mike Rutherford, released in Dec. 1988 in the UK and in Jan. 1989 in the US, cassette single.
31. Isaac Watts, "When I Survey the Wondrous Cross," *Hymns and Spiritual Songs*, 1707.
32. Maltbie Davenport Babcock, "This Is My Father's World," poem published in 1901, set to music in 1915 by Franklin L. Sheppard.
33. Thomas Chisholm, "Great Is Thy Faithfulness," set to music by William M. Runyan, published by Hope Publishing Company in 1923.
34. Karolina Wilhelmina Sandell-Berg, "Day by Day," 1858?, music by Oscar Ahnfelt, translated into English from Swedish by Andrew L. Skoog.
35. Chris Rice, "Smellin' Coffee," *Past the Edges*, Rocket Records label, released September 15, 1998.
36. John C. Maxwell, *The 21 Irrefutable Laws of Leadership: Follow Them and People Will Follow You* (Nashville: Thomas Nelson Inc., 1998, 2007).
37. Elaine Bruner and Phyllis Haddox, *Teach Your Child to Read in 100 Easy Lessons* (New York: Touchstone Books, 1986).
38. Corrie Ten Boom, *The Hiding Place, 35th Anniversary Edition* (Grand Rapids, MI: Chosen, 2006).
39. Tam Spiva, "Hawaii Bound," "Pass the Tabu," and "The Tiki Caves," *Brady Bunch*, copyright 1972, Season 4, Episodes 1-3, Production Numbers 073-075, Airdates: September 22, September 29, and October 6, 1972, directed by Jack Arnold.
40. Linda Ellis, "The Dash," copyright 1996, http://lindaellis.net/the-dash/the-dash-poem-by-linda-ellis/.
41. Tim Nichols and Craig Wiseman, "Live Like You Were Dying," *Live Like You Were Dying*, Curb label, recorded by Tim McGraw, produced by Byron Gallimore and Tim McGraw, released June 7, 2004, compact disc.
42. Karolina Wilhelmina Sandell-Berg, "Day by Day," 1858?, music by Oscar Ahnfelt, translated into English from Swedish by Andrew L. Skoog.
43. Kathrina Von Schlegel, "Be Still My Soul," music composed by Jean Sibelius, 1752, translated by Jane Borthwick and published in *Hymns from the Land of Luther* in 1855.
44. "Wet Oatmeal Kisses," Googol Learning, http://www.googolpower/content/free-learning-resources/inspiration, accessed August 28, 2013.
45. Nancy Leigh DeMoss, *Lies Women Believe: And the Truth that Sets Them Free* (Chicago: Moody Press, 2001).
46. Paul David Tripp, *The Age of Opportunity: A Biblical Guide to Parenting Teens* (Phillipsburg, NJ: Presbyterian and Reformed Publishing Company, 2001).
47. Chris Brady and Orrin Woodward, *LIFE* (Flint, MI: Obstaclés Press, 2011), 12.
48. Israel Houghton and New Breed, "Again I Say Rejoice," *Live from Another Level*, Integrity/Columbia label, released May 4, 2004.
49. Rick Warren, *Purpose Driven Life* (Grand Rapids, MI: Zondervan, 2002).
50. Anne Graham Lotz, *The Magnificent Obsession: Embracing the God-Filled Life* (Grand Rapids, MI: Zondervan, 2009), 23.
51. Ibid, 55.
52. "Sunrise, Sunset," *Fiddler on the Roof*, music by Jerry Bock, lyrics by Sheldon Harnick, first performance September 22, 1964.

About the Author

TERRI BRADY

An engineer in a former life, Terri now enjoys engineering a home with three buffaloes and a butterfly along with her #1 fan, *New York Times* bestselling author Chris Brady. Although a leadership speaker to tens of thousands around the world, business owner, and author of the popular blog *Letters to Lindsey*, her favorite title is "Mom," and she can usually be found cheering on the sidelines of a soccer field. She has an insatiable love for music, is solar-powered, and is known to be persuaded by chocolate and coffee. A brain tumor survivor, she seeks most to glorify God through His Son and enjoy Him forever.

Blogs - English: terribradyblog.com, LettersToLindsey.com
Blog- Spanish: cartasalindsey.wordpress.com
Facebook Page: Letters To Lindsey
X *(Formerly Twitter)*: X.com/TerriMBrady

ALL GRACE OUTREACH

All Grace Outreach originally began in 1993 in Maine as "Christian Mission Services." In March of 2007, the organization was transferred to Michigan, and the name was changed to All Grace Outreach. All Grace Outreach is a 501(c)3 charitable organization, which means all contributions are tax deductible. All Grace Outreach is committed to providing assistance to those in need. Our main focus is spreading the gospel of Jesus Christ throughout the world and helping abused, abandoned, and distressed children and widows.